Economic and Social Commission for Western Asia (ESCWA)

ESCWA Water Development Report 6

The water, energy and food security nexus in the Arab region

United Nations
Beirut

E/ESCWA/SDPD/2015/2
ISSN. 1817-1990
ISBN: 978-92-1-128380-8
e-ISBN. 978-92-1-057634-5
15-00339

UNITED NATIONS PUBLICATION
Sales No. E.16.II.L.1

CONTENTS

List of Tables

List of Figures

List of Boxes

List of Maps

Abbreviations

AMCE	Arab Ministerial Council on Electricity
AMWC	Arab Ministerial Water Council
AOAD	Arab Organization for Agricultural Development
BCM	Billion cubic metres
BGR	Federal Institute for Geosciences and Natural Resources
BMZ	Bundesministerium für wirtschaftliche Zusammenarbeit und Entwicklung (Federal Ministry for Economic Cooperation and Development)
CAMRE	Council of Arab Ministers Responsible for the Environment
CEDAW	Convention on the Elimination of All Forms of Discrimination Against Women
CFA	Cooperative Framework Agreement
CI	Continental Intercalaire
CLEW	Climate, land, energy, and water
CPV	Concentrated photovoltaics
CSP	Concentrated solar power
DESA	Department of Economic and Social Affairs
ECDPM	European Centre for Development Policy Management
ECE	Economic Commission for Europe
ESCWA	Economic and Social Commission for Western Asia
FAO	Food and Agriculture Organization of the United Nations
FO	Forward osmosis
FR	Fresnel reflector
GAP	Southeastern Anatolia Project
GCC	Gulf Cooperation Council
GCCIA	Gulf Cooperation Council Interconnection Authority
GDI/DIE	German Development Institute/Deutsches Institut für Entwicklungspolitik
GDP	Gross domestic product
GIS	Geographic information system
GIZ	Deutsche Gesellschaft für Internationale Zusammenarbeit (GIZ) GmbH
GW	Gigawatt
GWP-Med	Global Water Partnership Mediterranean
Ha	Hectare
HCPV	High Concentrated Photovoltaic
IAEA	International Atomic Energy Agency
ICIMOD	International Centre for Integrated Mountain Development
IFAD	International Fund for Agricultural Development

IFPRI	International Food Policy Research Institute
IIASA	International Institute for Applied System Analysis
IISD	International Institute for Sustainable Development
IRENA	International Renewable Energy Agency
IWRM	Integrated Water Resources Management
K	Potassium
Koe	Kilogram of oil equivalent
KTH	Royal Institute of Technology (Sweden)
Kw	Kilowatt
LCOE	Levelized cost of electricity
MCM	Million cubic metres
MDG	Millennium Development Goal
MED	Multi-effect desalination
MENA	Middle East and North Africa
MJ	Megajoule
MoAW	Ministry of Agriculture and Water (Saudi Arabia)
MoWE	Ministry of Water and Electricity (Saudi Arabia)
MoU	Memorandum of understanding
MSF	Multi-stage flash
MW	Megawatt
MWI	Ministry of Water and Irrigation (Jordan)
N	Nitrogen
NBI	Nile Basin Initiative
NEPCO	National Electric Power Company (Jordan)
NGO	Non-governmental organization
NWSAS	North-Western Sahara Aquifer System
ODI	Overseas Development Institute
OHCHR	Office of the United Nations High Commissioner for Human Rights
OSS	Observatory for Sahara and the Sahel
P	Phosphate
PT	Parabolic trough
PV	Photovoltaic (solar)
RBA	Rights-based approach to development
RO	Reverse osmosis
SD	Solar dish
SDC	Swiss Agency for Development and Cooperation
SDG	Sustainable Development Goal
SE4All	Sustainable Energy for All
SEI	Stockholm Environment Institute
Sida	Swedish International Development Cooperation Agency
ST	Solar tower
TADCO	Tabuk Agricultural Development Company

TCF	Trillion cubic feet
TVC	Thermal vapour compression
UNDP	United Nations Development Programme
UNEP	United Nations Environment Programme
UNIDO	United Nations Industrial Development Organization
UNU	United Nations University
WBCSD	World Business Council for Sustainable Development
WEF	Water-energy-food
WEL	Water-energy-land
WHO	World Health Organization

Executive summary

The sixth Water Development Report of the Economic and Social Commission for Western Asia (ESCWA) provides an analytical framework to help understand the water-energy-food security nexus in the Arab region. It considers climate change and the interlinkages that affect the achievement of of water- energy-food (WEF) security and advances a human rights approach to the Post-2015 Sustainable Development Goals to ensure access to food, water and sustainable energy for all.

Arab States arguably have much to gain from considering the interlinkages between water, energy and food security in their pursuit of sustainable development given the stressors, constraints and strong interdependencies that characterize the relationships between these three sectors in the region. Applying the framework at various scales of analysis across the three sectors can help understand complex relationships between these three sectors and considers the existing production and consumption patterns of natural resources in the region.

A nexus conceptual approach for the Arab region should take into consideration the scale of analysis and existing institutional and policy frameworks. It should also consider the ways in which technology can improve the ability to achieve water, energy and food security in a more efficient and integrated manner that is people-centred and based on human rights. The proposed analytical framework builds upon existing policy instruments and initiatives, including integrated water resources management, sustainable energy for all and the promotion of sustainable agriculture and trade within the context of climate change. It can also help tackle complex challenges that obstruct water, energy and food security, including shared water resources management and decision-making related to energy efficiency, in order to achieve food security despite water scarcity, land degradation and development objectives.

Applying the water-energy-food security nexus in the Arab region requires a vision based on shared principles that can be accepted by all Arab countries despite differences in their natural resources and socioeconomic capital. Therefore, the proposed analytical framework is set within the context of achieving sustainable development goals and can be applied through a set of human rights-based principles to ensure water, energy and food security for all.

This report reviews different nexus approaches, the importance of focusing on a specific scale of analysis, and the implications that a human rights approach to sustainable development can have on available policy space to ensure water, energy and food security for all. Through regional case studies, it introduces the regional institutional framework and associated nexus-related initiatives in the Arab region, examines the water-energy- security nexus from a shared-water-resources perspective and presents how this approach can support the management of shared surface water basins and groundwater resources. It provides an overview of the interlinkages within the WEF nexus for improved service delivery and the support of the agriculture sector by examining water use and efficiency in the production of energy and energy-intensive fertilizers, and the available technological options. It also examines the importance of trade, investment and sustainable agricultural policies in order to ensure food security in the region.

The report draws on conclusions and recommendations and reviews regional initiatives being implemented to help Arab States to better understand the water-energy-food security nexus as an analytical approach to sustainable development.

The WEF security nexus analytical framework, with its holistic approach, is well suited for the Arab region. It can assist in informing decision makers of synergies for achieving sustainable development from a people-centred approach to development based on universal human rights' principles that can provide a common denominator for dialogue and decision-making across ministries and countries.

Combining the WEF components with a view to the dynamics caused by climate change and the need to ensure access to such basic human rights as the right to food, water, sanitation and development, among others, with regional specificities, the WEF security nexus can provide an effective analytical framework that can assist Arab States achieve the desired progress towards sustainable development.

Introduction

Over the last few years, the links between the water, energy and food sectors have been examined under the water-energy-food (WEF) security nexus. In their pursuit of sustainable development, Arab States[1] have much to gain from a WEF nexus approach; however, it will require integrated thinking if WEF security is to be achieved at all levels across the Arab region.

The versatility of the nexus analytical framework is advantageous in that it can be applied at various scales of analysis to accommodate varying existing natural resources among the States. In terms of water security, Arab States are among the most water scarce in the world. 18 out of 22 Arab States fall below the renewable water scarcity annual threshold of 1,000 m^3 per capita, with 13 member States below the absolute water scarcity threshold of 500 m^3 per capita per year.[2] The total renewable water resources available in the region for the year 2014 ranged from as low as 5.9 m^3/capita/year in Kuwait to 2,931 m^3/capita/year in Mauritania.[3] This situation is exacerbated by the dependency on transboundary water resources, declining water quality, accessibility constraints due to occupation and conflict, climate change, non-revenue water losses, inefficient use of water and high population growth rates. There are also nearly 55 million people in the Arab region without access to an improved drinking water source, and nearly 66 million people without access to improved sanitation.[4] Furthermore, while over 56 per cent of the Arab region's population now lives in cities,[5] water for agriculture remains a priority to ensure food security and maintain rural livelihoods in the region's middle- and low-income countries, which is significant as the agricultural sector continues to consume nearly 80 per cent of the region's freshwater resources. Energy expenditures needed for desalination and pumping water from distant sources and deep groundwater aquifers add to the financial burden to ensure water security.

Numerous challenges facing food security in the Arab region are identical with those facing the water sector. Despite the technological advances that have improved agricultural productivity, efforts to achieve food security are complicated by natural resources depletion, fresh water scarcity, land degradation, high population growth, changing diets, economic development, and globalization, which has led Arab policymakers to the conclusion that food security cannot be achieved through food self-sufficiency alone. For instance, the 50 per cent increase in cereal production between 1990 and 2011 was still insufficient to meet demands, as evidenced by the 10 per cent increase in the region's cereal import dependency ratio over the same period.[6] Specifically, wheat production reached 28 million tons in 2013, representing a fivefold increase compared to the early 1960s; however, natural resources constraints and climate pressures have led most Arab countries to now importing a large share of their wheat.[7]

Several Arab countries have thus turned to international commodity trading and foreign land agreements to ensure food security and conserve scarce water resources while others have sought to expand their agricultural sectors in order to also generate income and support rural livelihoods.

Energy security is the third component to the WEF nexus, which, due to a divergence in the energy resources endowments and consumption patterns, is perceived differently by individual Arab States. For example, the Gulf Cooperation Council (GCC) countries[8] maintain high levels of energy consumption averaging 9,600 kg of oil equivalent per capita annually, in comparison to the remaining Arab countries that averaged 1,000 kg of oil equivalent per capita in 2011.[9] Energy consumption in the Arab region more than doubled between 1971 and 2011,[10] with energy consumption as a share of total primary regional energy production increasing from 25 per cent in 2001 to approximately 35 per cent in 2011.[11] This has serious implications on energy security and economic growth rates in the region. Rural electrification also remains a challenge in certain parts of the Arab region, together with electricity service intermittency and dependency on fuel imports, which, in turn, affect the ability to deliver reliable water services and ensure food safety in appropriate food storage and processing facilities. 65 per cent of the population in the Sudan and nearly 48 per cent in Yemen are not supplied with electricity, mostly in rural areas.[12] Accordingly, most Arab States seek to secure a more sustainable and diversified energy mix that includes renewable energy and increased energy efficiency.

The present report examines the WEF security nexus from the perspective of the Arab region. The nexus is presented as an analytical framework that can assist sustainable development in view of climate change and ensure the human right to food, water, sanitation, and development in the 2030 Development Agenda. It highlights the institutional frameworks and technological options that are available, in order to support Arab States in applying the nexus approach and to draw upon existing approaches and initiatives being implemented in the Arab region.

The report furthermore aims to introduce an analytical framework that can encourage policymakers and stakeholders to consider the implications of achieving security in one sector can have on resource sustainability and security targets in other sectors. It does so by signaling the challenges and benefits of intersectoral institutional frameworks and the need for more integrated and informed cross-sectoral dialogue and policymaking. However, Arab States and stakeholders need the political will to foster and institutionalize the necessary intergovernmental and cross-sectoral collaborative process to support the development of coordinated strategies and coherent policies under a nexus framework aimed at ensuring access to water, energy and food for all.

The report consists of five chapters. Chapter I presents the nexus as an analytical framework in varying scales of analysis and security dimensions. It also reviews the evolution of the nexus concept and offers a framework for applying a WEF security nexus in the Arab region. Chapter II examines the WEF security nexus from a shared water resources perspective by presenting case studies of how a nexus approach can help to better support the management of shared surface water basins and groundwater resources in the region. Chapter III provides an overview of the interlinkages between water and energy for improved service delivery by examining water use in energy and electricity production and the technology options available for improved WEF security in the delivery of water services and support to the agriculture sector. Chapter IV looks at food security from a nexus perspective by examining, among others, energy-intensive fertilizer production and the available technologies in the agriculture sector in order to increase water and energy use efficiency. The use of foreign trade and investment to ensure food security is also addressed in this chapter. The final chapter, Chapter V, draws conclusions from the report and reviews regional activities being implemented by the Economic and Social Commission for Western Asia (ESCWA) and its partners to support Arab States in operationalizing the WEF security nexus as a means to support progress towards sustainable development in the Arab region.

I. Framing the Water-Energy-Food Security Nexus

This chapter highlights the extent to which the WEF security nexus can serve as an effective analytical framework in support of sustainable development in the Arab region. The nexus approach enables broad analysis taking into account security and a human rights-based approach to development from an integrated perspective. It makes it possible to look at synergies, the use of appropriate technologies and issues such as climate change, population growth and urbanization, changes in production and consumption patterns, and ecosystem degradation.

A. Understanding the nexus

A nexus conceptual framework can help to identify links between the water, energy and food sectors, with a view to achieving integrated natural resources management. The use of such a framework can help to better understand sustainable development challenges in the Arab region.

1. Origins of the nexus concept

The nexus has existed under various forms for decades. Integrated natural resources management, integrated water resources management (IWRM), sustainable agriculture, green economy principles, sustainable

production and consumption frameworks, and sustainable development itself are all based on a nexus concept aimed at improving the management of natural resources and associated ecosystems. Early on, IWRM promoted an integrated approach based on the principles articulated in the Dublin Statement on Water and Sustainable Development of 1992 (box 1), and an action agenda focused on poverty, disease, natural disasters, urban and rural water supply, agriculture, ecosystems, and the resolution of water conflicts. Those principles take a people-centred and participatory approach to development, highlighting the central role of women in the provision, management and safeguarding of water for achieving IWRM. However, the formulation of IWRM strategies and plans failed to garner the cross-sectoral support needed to move the concept beyond the water box.

The adoption of the Millennium Declaration in 2000 and its operationalization through the Millennium Development Goals (MDGs) represented a shift in thinking about integrated natural resources management. While the Millennium Declaration called for the respect for nature and the prudent management of all living species and natural resources according to the precepts of sustainable development, Goal 7 set a 15-year programme of action on environmental sustainability aimed at reversing the loss of environmental resources, improving access to water supply and sanitation services, reducing biodiversity loss, and improving the lives of slum dwellers, while encouraging States to adopt IWRM plans by the year 2005. In doing so, Goal 7 was successful in linking sustainable natural resources management to the provisions of basic services, namely water supply and sanitation, under the sustainability umbrella.

The importance of linking integrated natural resources management to WEF security became apparent with the global financial crisis and the concurrent food and energy crises of 2007 and 2008. This was complemented by growing concern about the dwindling natural resources base, water scarcity, increasing land degradation, and mounting scientific evidence that human activities are pushing the Earth's natural systems beyond sustainable limits and are contributing to climate change.

The nexus thus emerged as a conceptual framework that highlights the interdependencies between the water, energy and food sectors, and the need to pursue an integrated management framework across these three sectors if sustainable development is to be achieved. The value of a nexus conceptual framework thus arises from its ability to focus attention on the interdependencies between issues related to water, energy and food from a cross-sectoral perspective that incorporates the management of both sustainable natural resources and adequate access to food, water and sustainable energy for all.

2. Overview of different nexus approaches

Traditionally, nexus relationships have highlighted two-way relationships, such as energy needed for water supply, or water needed for irrigation. They have also been focused on improving the sustainable management of natural resources. More recently, more complex nexus approaches have emerged in which at least three sectors are considered from the point of view of resource management and service delivery.

Nexus constructs vary depending on scope, goals and appreciation of the drivers affecting at least three core sectors. A modular approach to nexus frameworks has emerged, which allows the incorporation of additional issues into the core triangle. This section illustrates some of the variations that have emerged in order to help clarify the nexus approach, and which may be characterized by the clusters illustrated in figure 1.

Figure 1. Selected conceptual frameworks for illustrating the natural resource nexus

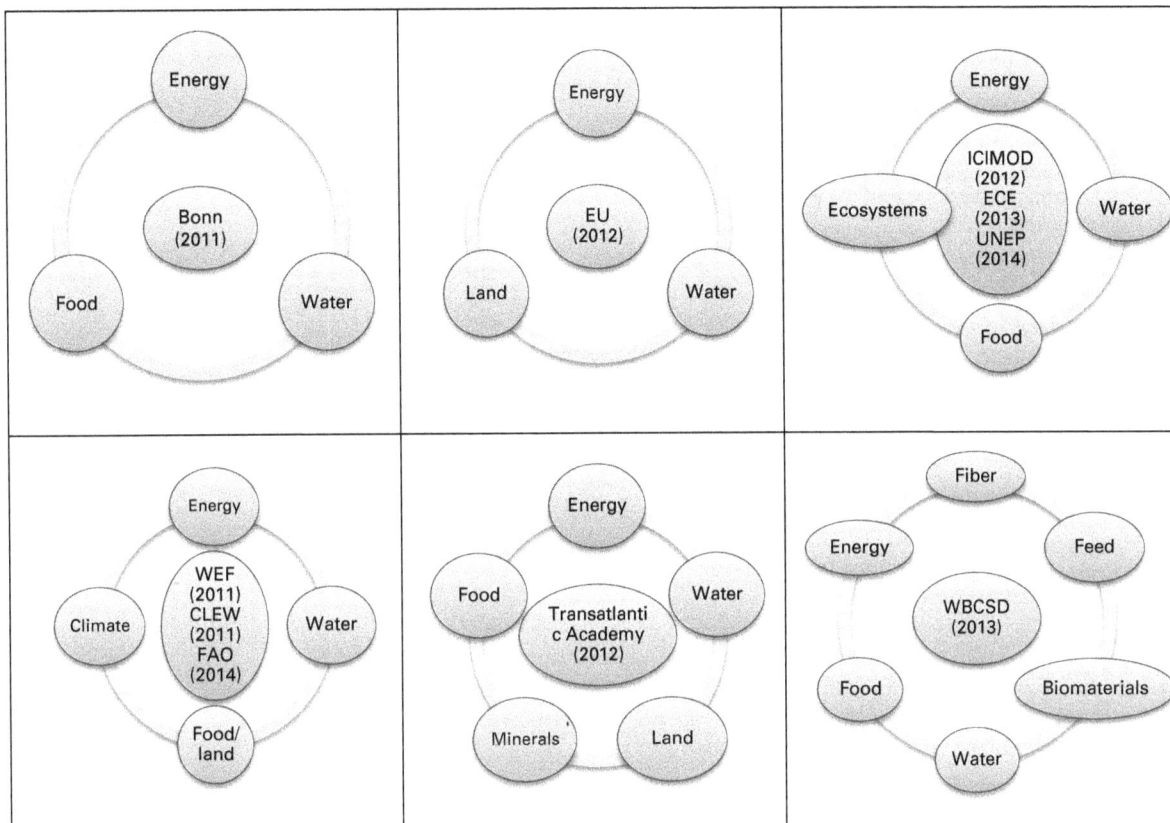

Source: ESCWA, 2015b.

Note: EU stands for European Union, ICIMOD for International Centre for Integrated Mountain Development; ECE for Economic Commission for Europe; UNEP for United Nations Environment Programme; WEF for World Economic Forum; CLEW for Climate, land, energy and water; FAO for Food and Agriculture Organization; and WBCSD for World Business Council for Sustainable Development.

(a) Water-energy-food nexus

A background paper by the Stockholm Environment Institute (SEI) for the Bonn 2011 Nexus Conference (figure 2) placed available water resources at the centre of the nexus since the people involved in the production of the paper mainly originated from the water sector.

The model identified urbanization, population growth and climate change as global drivers and society, economy and environment as fields requiring action.

This approach also emphasized the importance of governance and policy coherency and recognized finance and innovation as enabling factors. The importance of international trade in supporting global food security was also highlighted, with specific reference made to Middle East and North Africa (MENA).[13] However, the paper fails to suggest a pathway for defining security within a global or regional context and is unclear on how to reconcile resource efficiency to ensure WEF security for all.

Figure 2. The water-energy-food security nexus (Bonn 2011)

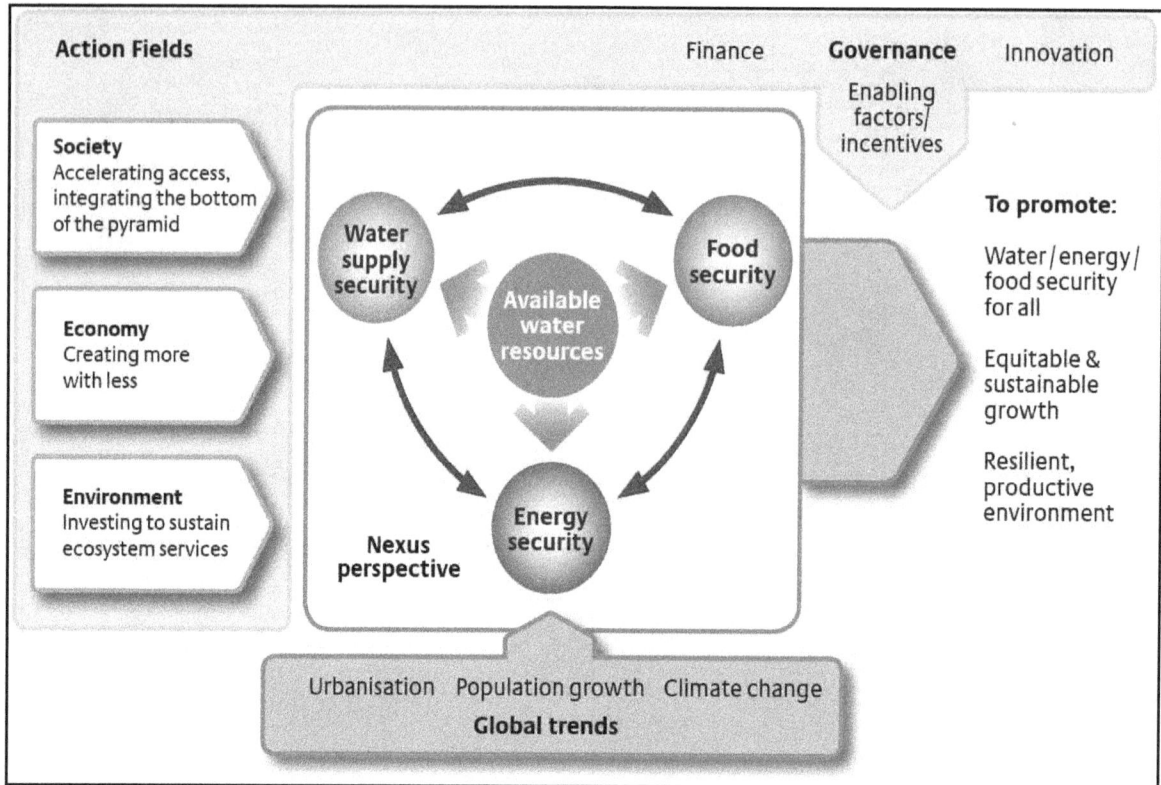

Source: Hoff, 2011.

Nevertheless, the SEI approach is unique in that it clearly identifies universal access to water, energy and food as a goal, alongside equitable and sustainable growth within a resilient and productive environment, which is a valuable dimension to consider during the construction of a nexus conceptual framework within the context of the 2030 Development Agenda.

(b) Water-energy-land nexus

The water-energy-land (WEL) nexus, presented in the 2011/2012 European Report on Development,[14] substitutes the food sector component with land and land-based natural resources, which include competing land uses and needs for forests, biodiversity, agriculture, and human settlements (figure 3).

The main aim is to promote growth that is socially inclusive and environmentally sustainable by transforming the management of natural resources. Four key areas of action are identified, which include modifying demand patterns to match natural resources availability, improving the quantity and quality of supply and increasing efficiency and resilience. However, the WEL nexus fails to sufficiently elaborate on the energy component and remains largely centred on the management of water and land resources.

Figure 3. The water-energy-land nexus

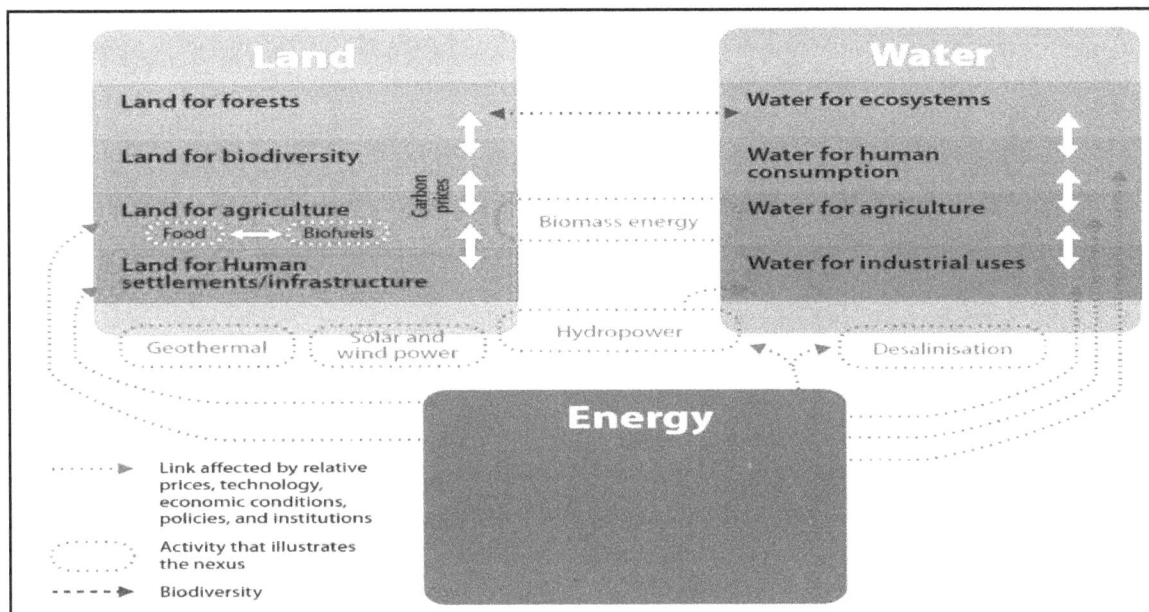

Figure 4. The water-energy-food-ecosystems nexus

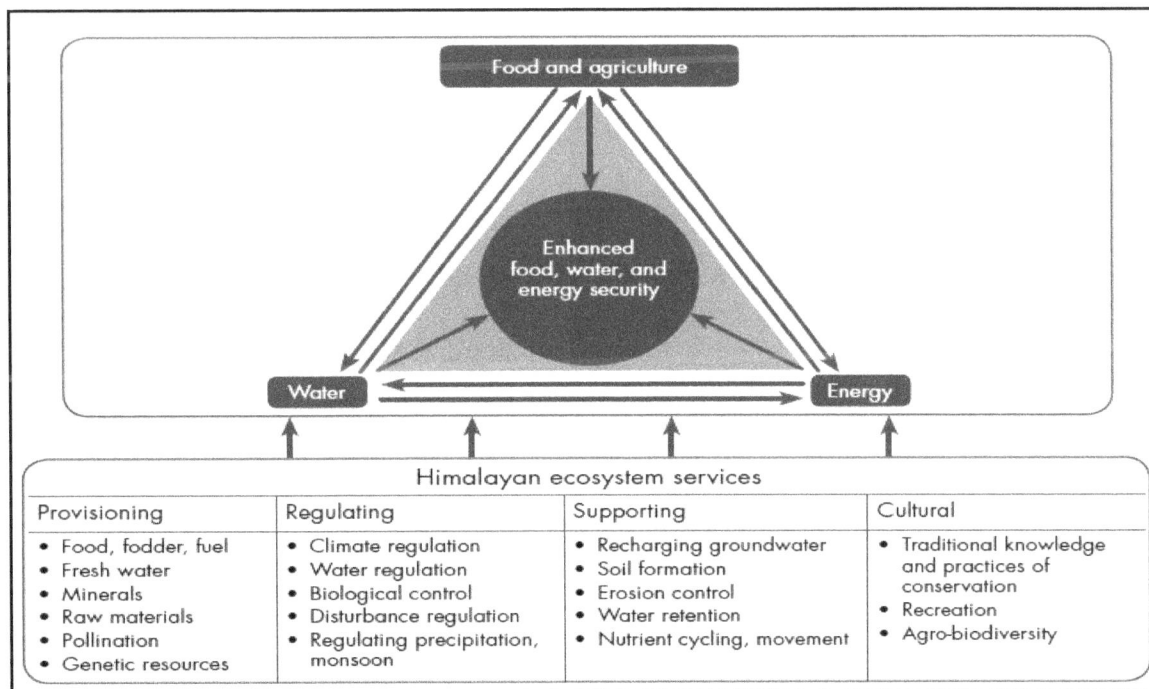

(c) Water-energy-food-ecosystems nexus

Three conceptual frameworks that support a water-energy-food-ecosystems nexus approach are provided by the International Centre for Integrated Mountain Development (ICIMOD), the United Nations Economic Commission for Europe (ECE), and the United Nations Environment Programme (UNEP). The ICIMOD nexus framework was initially applied to the Himalayas and South Asia and focuses on the ecosystem of goods and services in order to support the food, water and energy sectors (figure 4). It includes the restoration of natural water storage capacities, the development of a climate-smart and socially sound infrastructure and the introduction of incentive mechanisms for managing ecosystems.

The UNEP nexus places the organization at the centre of the three sectors (figure 5). The framework includes land as an added dimension and views climate change as an external stressor on ecosystems and associated components. It recognizes the potential benefits of a nexus approach for basin organizations that aim to improve water governance while ensuring energy and food security, specifically through the production of hydropower and biofuel.

ECE positions the WEF nexus within the context of ecosystems and acknowledges that development objectives should not compromise the ecosystem. The framework recognizes weaknesses in intersectoral coordination as major challenges at the basin level, resulting in the potential for conflict between riparian countries and associated interest groups. The ECE approach to conducting nexus assessments is largely based on structuring consultative processes and knowledge sharing.[15] This framework has been used as a basis for conducting assessments of the water-food-energy-ecosystem nexus on a number of transboundary basins in 2015, with plans underway to conduct a similar nexus assessment of the North West Sahara Aquifer.[16]

(d) Climate-land-energy-water nexus

The climate, land, energy and water (CLEW) nexus advanced by the World Economic Forum was introduced in 2011 and stems from a global risk perspective that was largely geopolitical and economic in scope. This approach was applied within the Jordanian context, with the support of the Jordanian Ministry of Planning and International Cooperation and the Ministry of Water and Irrigation.[17]

Figure 5. The ecosystem nexus

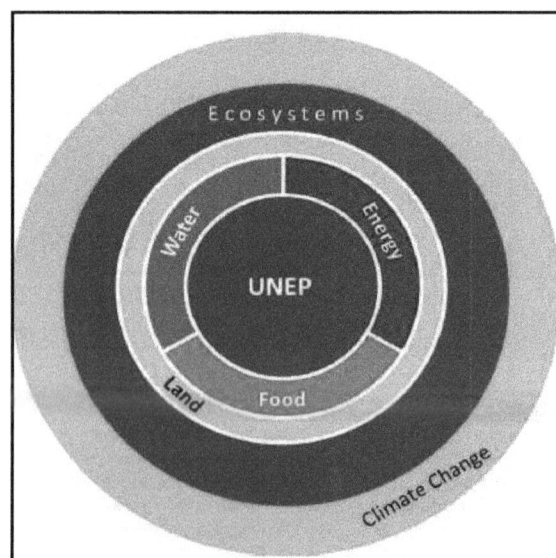

Source: Boelee, Hoa and Chiramba, 2014.

It presents population and economic growth and environmental pressures – mainly climate change – as major stressors affecting the WEF nexus. It identified global governance failures and economic disparity as risks that could lead to system failures and conflict if WEF security were not taken into consideration (figure 6).

The Food and Agriculture Organization of the United Nations (FAO) presented a different CLEW nexus, which centralizes stakeholder dialogue (figure 7). From the perspective of food security and sustainable agriculture, the framework adopts a holistic approach, specifically within human and natural systems interaction. The drivers affecting the nexus include demographic changes, industrial and agricultural development, global trade, technology and innovation, urbanization, changing diets, climate change, and governance structures and processes. To achieve WEF goals, the resource base includes land, water, energy, capital and labour, with FAO identifying evidence, scenario development and response options as three areas to manage and assess nexus interactions.

Figure 6. System diagram for risks associated with the water-energy-food nexus

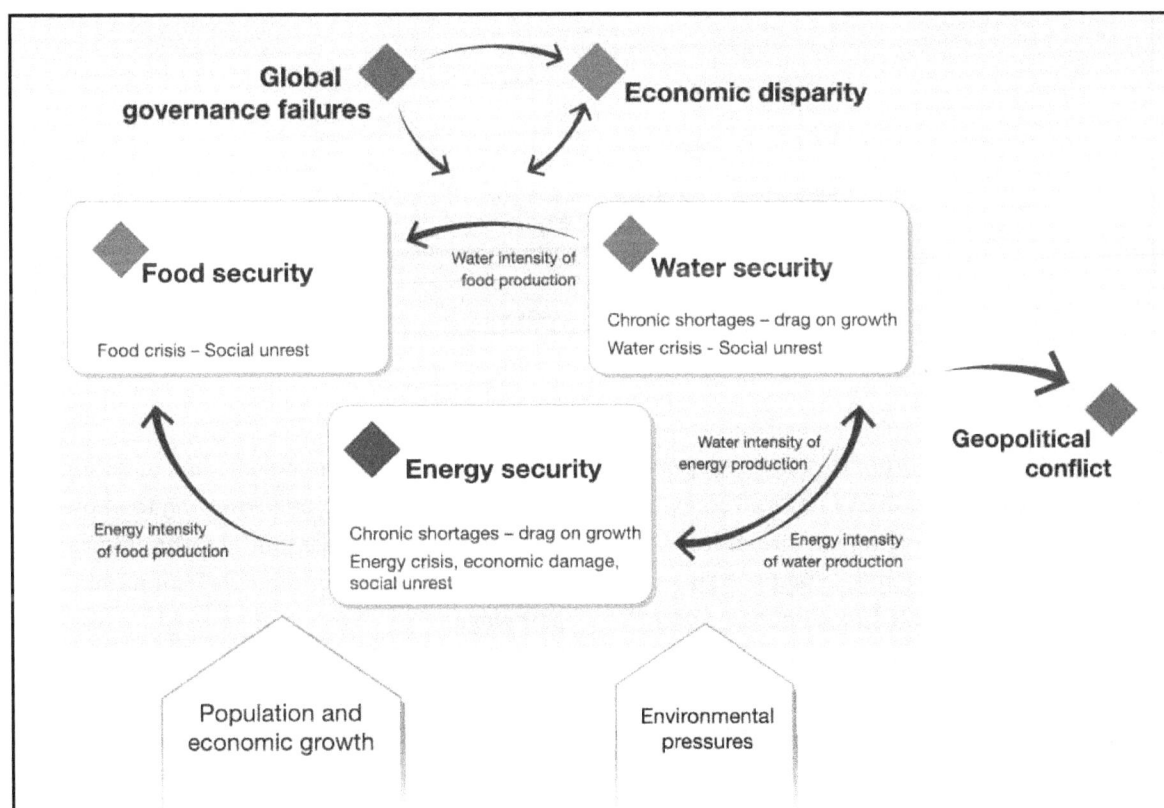

Source: World Economic Forum, 2011.

Figure 7. The FAO approach to the water-energy-food nexus

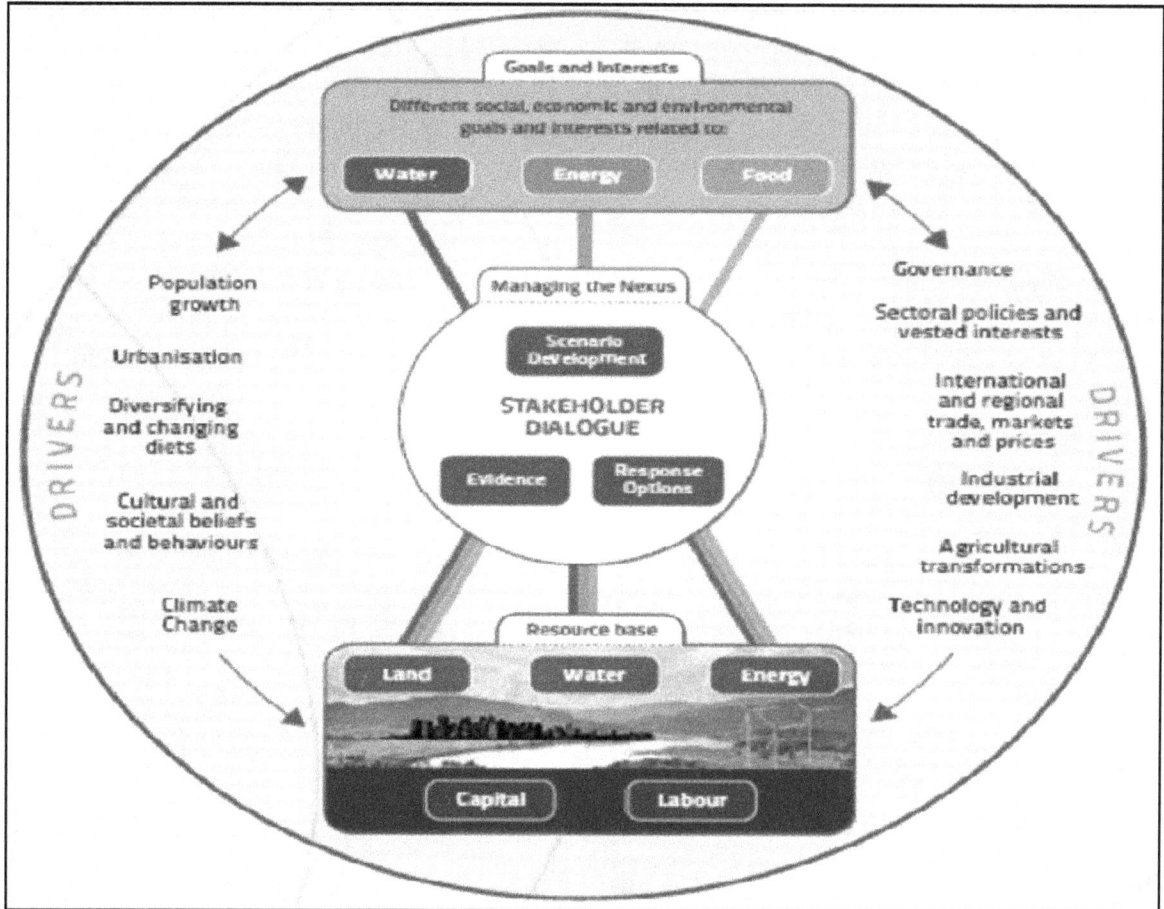

Several international organizations and research centres have modeled CLEW nexus frameworks, with land as the underlying constraint for examining food and climate change.[18] This quantitative approach focuses on integrating water and energy planning and agroecological zoning models. It is further complicated by considering the relationship between land, energy, water, and climate with the importance of efficient resource management, and feedback loops and interdependencies between the different resources within the context of climate change. The CLEW approach aims to support decision-making and policymaking to allow a more inclusive assessment of technological options and socioeconomic development pathways.

(e) Water-energy-food-land-minerals nexus

The water-energy-food-land-minerals nexus framework focuses on five resources, which can experience market fluctuations and lead to violent conflicts. Presented by the Transatlantic

Academy, this approach suggests that the association between the production and consumption of these resources is the basis for the global economy and exhibits threats associated with a disrupted global supply chain, market volatility, poverty, and declining human security. The framework identifies several opportunities that address security risks, including resource efficiency, sustainable development, greener growth, institutional building, and engaged cooperation. It also takes note of food import dependencies – particularly in countries of the Middle East and North Africa – as creating a new geography for commodities trading and a potential threat to international security.[19]

(f) Water-energy-food-feed-fibre-biomaterials nexus

The water-energy-food-feed-fibre-biomaterials nexus, a private-sector initiative developed by the World Business Council for Sustainable Development (WBCSD), aims to provide optimized solutions to benefit the WEF sectors while incorporating feed and fertilizers (figure 8). Keeping in mind the impacts on climate, this approach requires closing the knowledge gap and identifies opportunities that include clever crop agronomy, varieties of smart seeds, mixed farming systems, improved blue and green water productivity, efficient fertilizer production, farm operation and mechanization, and reduction of waste.

The inclusion of fertilizer production and consumption in this framework is of particular interest for the Arab region, which is a significant producer of phosphate and nitrogen fertilizers.

Figure 8. Conceptual layout of the WBCSD water-energy- food-feed-fibre-climate nexus

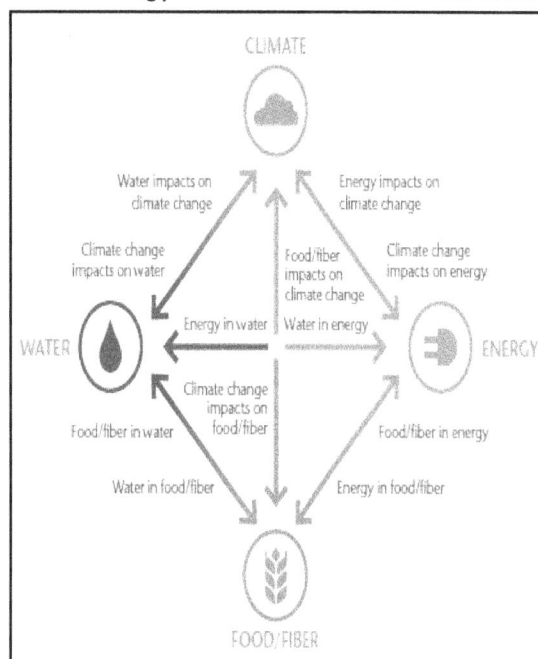

Source: WBCSD, 2013.

(g) Additional nexus frameworks

The schematic framework of the WEF nexus presented in figure 2 is not all-inclusive but reflects the dominant conceptual frameworks and methodologies promoted by various organizations. There are numerous other variations that may or may not fit the configuration of nexus elements, including those presented below.

The International Institute for Sustainable Development (IISD) nexus approach is another framework centred on ecosystem management. It identifies several key elements for achieving WEF security (figure 9). Providing an implementation-focused process with ecosystems and restoration management services at the watershed-scale, the multilevel analysis focuses on the utilization of resources, starting with three independent security frameworks for WEF. Further analysis identifies how watershed communities access these resources, using both natural and human-built systems. This analytical framework is embedded within a participatory planning process and includes four stages: assessing the WEF nexus; envisioning future landscape scenarios; investing in a WEF-secure future; and transforming the system.

The nexus approach by the Federal Ministry for Economic Cooperation and Development (Bundesministerium für wirtschaftliche Zusammenarbeit und Entwicklung (BMZ)) of Germany originates in the need for efficient, cross-sectoral resource management of urban sustainable development. BMZ provides several solutions that include the development of

sustainable relationships between urban agri-food consumer markets and the surrounding rural areas; the management of urban and social mobility in order to lessen conflict over land use; the improvement of microclimates through the management of urban green spaces; and the increasing of resource productivity and reduction of waste with a view to generating economic and environmental gains while reducing consumption across sectors.[20] The BMZ has also been promoting the conduct of nexus dialogues in various parts of the world, including in the Arab region. A more extensive review of these and other nexus approaches is available in the ESCWA Working Paper on Conceptual Frameworks for Understanding the Water, Energy and Food Security Nexus.

Figure 9. Overview of the IISD nexus framework

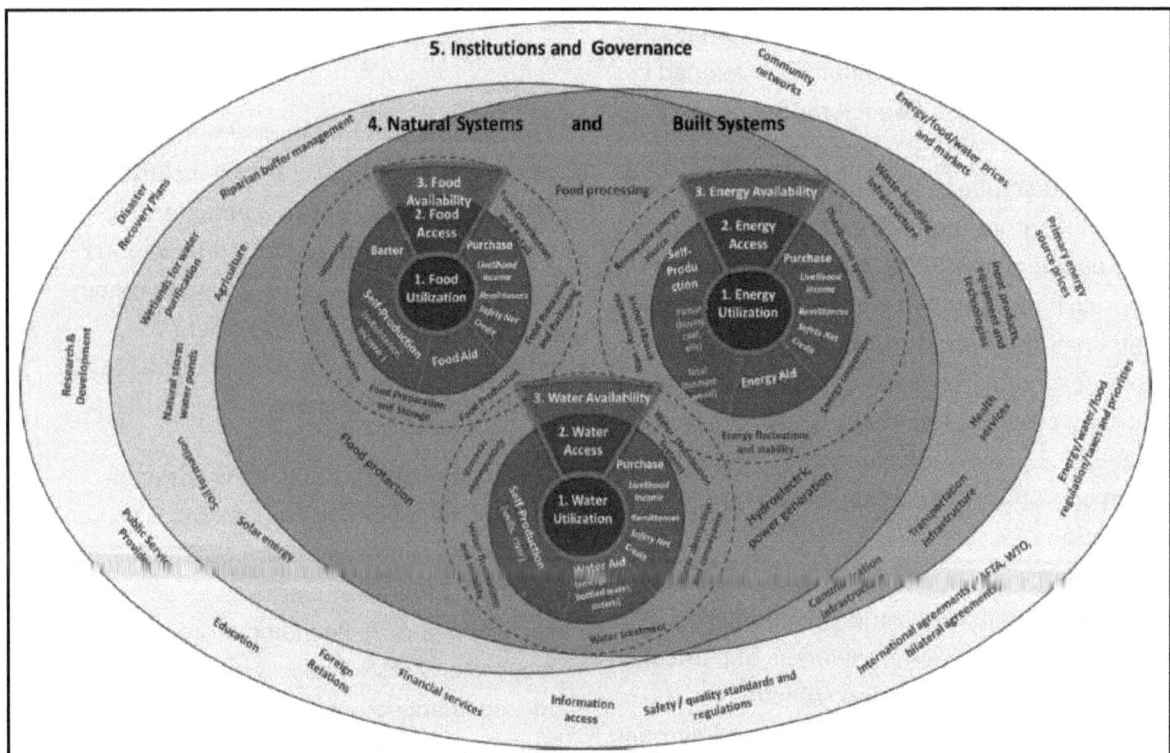

Source: Bizikova, and others, 2013.

B. Elaborating a water-energy-food security nexus within the context of sustainable development

The above section reviews the main approaches for constructing a conceptual WEF-nexus framework and can be drawn upon to develop a WEF security nexus within the context of the 2030Development Agenda for the Arab region.

Some of the aforementioned approaches focus on the WEF nexus from an economic perspective (for instance, the World Economic Forum), others focus on ecosystems (for instance, UNEP, ECE and IISD), or on the natural resource base (for instance, the EU). Several approaches consider such drivers as climate change and population growth (for instance, SEI and WBCSD). Additionally, certain institutions have constructed complex approaches that integrate such dimensions as minerals or feedstock (for instance, WBCSD) or specific implementation instruments, such as stakeholder consultation and other participatory approaches (for instance, FAO and IISD). However, only the World Economic Forum and SEI refer to a WEF security nexus that explicitly mentions the conditions of Arab countries in their analysis. Therefore, the dominate influences of these two approaches are drawn upon when constructing the nexus conceptual framework for the Arab region.

However, the formulation of a nexus conceptual framework in a 2030Development Agenda context for the Arab region requires consideration of three additional factors. These include setting the scale and scope of the desired conceptual approach; considering the institutional and policy frameworks and associated principles against which decisions should be taken; and reflecting on the instruments available to support the implementation of policies that may have competing aims. These three components are elaborated in the sections below and set the backdrop for formulating a nexus conceptual framework for the Arab region within the context of the 2030Development Agenda.

1. Scale and scope of analysis

One advantage of a nexus approach is its flexibility, which enables broad analysis focusing on generating policies and interventions. Analysis can vary from the global and regional macrolevel scale to the national and local microlevel scale, ranging from policies, plans and strategies to measures, actions and interventions. Interactions that influence the WEF security links are then defined by scale and scope in applying a nexus approach to a policy problem as detailed below.

- Global level: The WEF security nexus includes issues related to climate change, trade flows and financial regimes, technology transfer and the formulation of development priorities, such as the Sustainable Development Goals (SDGs) defined in the 2030Development Agenda;
- Regional level: In addition to the issues at the global level, analysis focuses more on regional specificities, such as natural resource endowments, international labour, migration and refugee flows, geopolitics, and arrangements to foster regional integration and inter-State cooperation, which directly affect the ability of States to budget the natural, financial and human resources. As

the potential of a State to ensure its WEF security is largely limited by its natural resource endowment, States need to pursue cooperation arrangements with external actors at intraregional and interregional levels to build national capacities and secure the resources they do not possess themselves;

- National and local levels: A nexus requires States to seek a balance between national security imperatives and policy dictates in order to satisfy the WEF needs of its citizens, with due consideration of universal human rights. The State must consider equity and redistributional aspects of the WEF security nexus, with special attention to non-discrimination and ensuring the right to water, food and sustainable energy for development across communities;

- Firm or household levels: The nexus presents a way for managers or heads of households to consider the sustainability aspects of their individual production and consumption practices from a WEF perspective. This often entails examining a series of bilateral relationships rather than framing a trilateral nexus, such as water-energy, food-energy and water-food interlinkages, within a combined nexus framework.

Ensuring WEF security at all these scales of analysis requires the setting of clear objectives and engagement with relevant stakeholders within the targeted system. As highlighted in the FAO and ECE approaches to the nexus, consultative and multi-stakeholder participatory approaches aimed at achieving consensus on common goals, identifying gaps and proposing solutions to ensure policy coherence across the designated scale for analysis are among the mechanisms sought for the operationalization of the nexus. It is indispensible that line ministries, institutions, non-governmental organization (NGOs) and local stakeholders pursue intersectoral collaboration despite the prevailing silo mentality evident throughout the world. Concerted efforts to achieve policy coherence are challenging, particularly when seeking to identify or pursue win-win solutions that entail an unequal allocation of benefits or prioritize one interest group above the other. Consultative processes and stakeholder engagement at the appropriate scale of analysis can thus help in identifying common goals and solutions that avoid one group of sectors or constituencies consistently suffering negative trade-offs relative to the others.

2. The institutional and policy framework for pursing a water-energy-food security nexus

The efforts of the various institutional frameworks when addressing links between the three elements of the WEF security nexus must be harmonized. Ministries tasked with water resources management may seek to advocate reductions in agricultural water use to conserve scarce water resources and achieve their definition of water security. Ministries of energy and electricity may be inattentive to the energy needs of water utilities responsible for water supply and sanitation services, especially during periods of peak energy demand or when energy prices are high. Ministries of agriculture tend to prioritize the water and energy needs of farming communities for food production and processing in light of the food security targets they wish to meet. However, none of these public sector institutions would admit that their work is counterproductive to national WEF security objectives.

The challenge thus lies in defining the WEF security nexus within an institutional framework that has divergent definitions of what constitutes security at the regional, national and sectoral levels. While identifying common security definitions at each level and in each sector may help, this is insufficient as security constructs may evolve over time and are influenced by the perceptions of the current state of affairs and the way in which countries and communities wish to frame their development priorities.

By contrast, a human rights-based approach to WEF security across the three sectors reflects the vision set forth in the new SDGs . A human rights-based approach can thus provide a common set of principles on which policy deliberations and positions can be based across institutions and sectors.

Furthermore, an analytical framework for examining the WEF security nexus from a people-centred approach is consistent with efforts to promote a human rights-based approach to development as adopted by the United Nations, which stipulates that the "human rights standards contained in, and principles derived from, the Universal Declaration of Human Rights and other international human rights instruments guide all development cooperation and programming in all sectors and in all phases of the programming process".[21]

Provision of basic human rights, including food and water, and the right to development, which

require access to energy, are core tenets of the human rights policy framework adopted by the member States of the United Nations. A number of resolutions have been adopted which support a human rights-based approach to the WEF security nexus within the context of ensuring water, energy and food for all.

The right to food has been acknowledged repeatedly, including by the United Nations General Assembly in the Universal Declaration of Human Rights;[22] the United Nations Committee on Economic, Social, and Cultural Rights;[23] and the Human Rights Council.[24]

These rights were also echoed at the World Summit on Food Security, which took place in Rome in 2009, and subsequent conferences, and followed up by the reformulated Committee on World Food Security. They are monitored by the Special Rapporteur on the Right to Food of the United Nations Human Rights Council.

With regard to the right to water, the United Nations Water Conference, held in Mar del Platain 1977, was the first world conference to declare that "all peoples, whatever their stage of development and social and economic conditions, have the right to have access to drinking water in quantities and of a quality equal to their basic needs".[25] This right was more forcefully elaborated in United Nations General Assembly resolution 64/292 (July 2010),[26] and United Nations Human Rights Council resolution 15/9 (October 2010).[27]

The right to development has been enshrined in many United Nations resolutions, most prominently in the United Nations General

Assembly Declaration on the Right to Development.[28] While the declaration, in Article 1, largely focuses on establishing the right to development as "an inalienable human right" that covers economic, social, cultural, and political development, Article 8 asserts that "States should undertake, at the national level, all necessary measures for the realization of the right to development and shall ensure, inter alia, equality of opportunity for all in their access to basic resources, education, health services, food, housing, employment and the fair distribution of income. Effective measures should be undertaken to ensure that women have an active role in the development process. Appropriate economic and social reforms should be carried out with a view to eradicating all social injustices."

Governments, however, have been hesitant to articulate access to energy and electricity services as a prerequisite for development due to the associated obligation of States to ensure access to energy as a universal human right and the implications that the associated increase in energy consumption would pose for national budgets and climate change. There is no United Nations resolution defining the human right to energy or electricity, although there are significant references to the need for energy to eradicate poverty and the importance of considering access to energy services within a human rights framework.[29]

However, the adoption of more sustainable energy practices for ensuring energy security have encouraged Governments and intergovernmental organs to articulate common goals regarding the need for energy for development. This led the United Nations Secretary-General to launch the Sustainable Energy for All (SE4All) initiative in September 2011.[30]

The SE4All initiative has three main objectives: (a) ensuring universal access to modern energy services; (b) doubling the global rate of improvement in energy efficiency; and (c) doubling the share of renewable energy in the global energy mix. Realizing these goals will result in rippling efficiency spillover effects across other sectors, such as water and food, with associated economic, social and environmental benefits that also contribute to climate change stabilization in the long term.

The global policy framework also pays special attention to the development rights of rural women, among others through the Convention on the Elimination of All Forms of Discrimination Against Women (CEDAW), which came into force in 1981. The Convention specifically calls on States to ensure that rural women have the right to "enjoy adequate living conditions, particularly in relation to housing, sanitation, electricity and water supply" (Article 14(h)).

(a) Implications of adopting a human rights-based approach to the water-energy-food security nexus

A human rights-based approach to development is grounded in a set of norms, principles, capacities, and obligations that consider human rights to be universal, indivisible, interdependent, and non-discriminatory. Therefore, as a visionary aim, this approach to the nexus should consider food, water, sanitation, and energy as inalienable rights that should be prioritized during policy formulation processes drawing upon a nexus analytical framework, particularly during the planning, implementation and monitoring of sustainable development and the SDGs in the 2030 Development Agenda. Enshrining access to food, water and sanitation, development and energy, inter alia, as universal human rights thus renders them core tenants of the WEF security nexus and sustainable development frameworks.

Nevertheless, setting priorities in policies, plans and budgets is highly complex when the right to food and water must be realized under consideration of each other and other universal rights, including the right to housing, health and well-being.[31] This is magnified when other policy goals are pursued, for instance, through military expenditures or efforts aimed at ensuring peace and security. A human rights-based approach to the WEF nexus would aim to prioritize the universality, indivisibility and interdependence of these basic human rights first and only then accommodate political exigencies.

The challenge of considering the need to secure universal human rights within the nexus is thus that it can constrain the policy space available to the decision makers. With access to food, water and sanitation enshrined as human rights, their achievement must be ensured for all. While the short- and long-term sequencing of human rights is politically necessary in face of resource constraints, their inclusion in development plans requires obligations by the State vis à vis its citizens, which should include mobilizing action, monitoring results and ensuring accountability. The trade-offs that are necessary

to be made with regard to these universal, indivisible and interdependent rights due to natural, financial or human resource constraints should be relative and still aim to provide for WEF security for all in a non-discriminatory manner.

(b) The water-energy-food security nexus within the context of human rights and Sustainable Development Goals

In preparation for the 2030Development Agenda, world leaders at the United Nations Conference on Sustainable Development (Rio+20) agreed to formulate SDGs with the aim to guide collective action beyond the year 2015. This vision was articulated in the Rio+20 outcome document "The future we want" and adopted by the United Nations General Assembly in September 2011. The document does not specifically refer to the nexus but does address the three core components of the nexus in consecutive sections, as summarized in box 2. These three clusters were subsequently taken up during the 2013-2014 deliberations of the Open Working Group on the SDGs, which led to the formulation of 17 SDGs.

Early deliberations on the formulation of the SDGs included advocates calling for a human rights-based approach to the 2030Development Agenda. However, certain Governments raised concerns regarding the inclusion of good governance precepts and fundamental freedoms in the language of the SDGs. Nevertheless, a human rights approach to the SDGs is manifested through the universality adopted 17 visionary goals that comprise the SDGs.

Box 2. The future we want

Food security and nutrition and sustainable agriculture

108. We reaffirm our commitments regarding the right of everyone to have access to safe, sufficient and nutritious food, consistent with the right to adequate food and the fundamental right of everyone to be free from hunger.

Water and sanitation

119. We recognize that water is at the core of sustainable development as it is closely linked to a number of key global challenges. We therefore reiterate the importance of integrating water into sustainable development, and underline the critical importance of water and sanitation within the three dimensions of sustainable development.

120. We commit to the progressive realization of access to safe and affordable drinking water and basic sanitation for all, as necessary for poverty eradication, women's empowerment and to protect human health, and to significantly improve the implementation of integrated water resource management at all levels as appropriate.

Energy

125. We recognize the critical role that energy plays in the development process, as access to sustainable modern energy services contributes to poverty eradication, saves lives, improves health and helps to provide for basic human needs. We stress that these services are essential to social inclusion and gender equality, and that energy is also a key input to production. We commit to facilitate support for access to these services by 1.4 billion people worldwide who are currently without them. We recognize that access to these services is critical for achieving sustainable development.

Source: United Nations General Assembly, 2012.

Specifically, the three components of the WEF security nexus are laid out in the following Goals:

- SDG 2, which seeks to "end hunger, achieve food security and improved nutrition and promote sustainable agriculture";
- SDG 6, which seeks to "ensure availability and sustainable management of water and sanitation for all";
- SDG 7, which seeks to "ensure access to affordable, reliable, sustainable and modern energy for all".

Positioning food security and universal access to water, sanitation and energy for all within the context of the SDGs requires States not only to consider universality as an important goal when ensuring water, food and energy today, but also encourages consideration of the implications of proposed policies, plans and measures between generations. A human rights perspective on the SDGs places the nexus in a dynamic context that considers the quantity, quality and accessibility of water, energy and food for present and future generations.

3. Contextualizing technology and efficiency in the nexus

Technology presents an important factor for increasing resource availability through efficiency improvements, the application of new knowledge or investments in new ways of doing business.

In terms of the nexus, technology can help to expand the available natural resource base in order to achieve WEF security. However, decision-making on the selection of technology options within a nexus framework should be focused on the designated scale of analysis and consider WEF security as prerequisites that may trump calculations aimed at achieving technical or economic efficiency alone.[32]

In the light of this challenge, a WEF security nexus approach prioritizes the security of all three sectors at the appropriate scale of analysis in the first instance by maximizing technical and economic efficiency. However, given the aforementioned preconditions that guide the prioritization of WEF security nexus policies, resource optimization should be sought, although this may result in the inability of a modeled nexus system to achieve technical or economic efficiency.

For instance, economic efficiency seeks to maximize output at the lowest production price. In monetary terms, this may result in the allocation of scarce water resources for oil exploration that is able to generate revenues in the short term instead of storing water for future generations or for use during disasters. A nexus model aimed at maximizing technical efficiency may determine that it is more efficient to only purchase food from abroad, despite national priorities aimed at supporting rural livelihoods or political exigencies associated with ensuring food security through self-sufficiency in a few strategic commodities in order to reduce risks related to price volatility and food import dependency.

A nexus conceptual framework aimed at maximizing economic efficiency may also advocate the reduction or entire deletion of water or energy subsidies, regardless of the possible socioeconomic costs for vulnerable groups. A purely economic efficiency approach to the nexus is thus generally counterproductive when assessing trade-offs that may affect different communities or countries, particularly if the right to food, water and energy for all is not incorporated in the calculation. The evaluation of technology options to achieve efficiency improvements within the WEF security nexus should thus not only aim at achieving efficiency gains, but be aligned with the human rights-based approach articulated in the SDGs.

C. A water-energy-food security nexus for the Arab region

Arab States have natural resource endowments that vary both between and within individual States. This affects the ability of States to achieve WEF security for their citizens and for foreign workers, migrants and refugees that often constitute vulnerable communities.

The WEF relationship in the region is also impacted by population dynamics, including high population growth, increasing urbanization and the associated socioeconomic disparities. Unsustainable production and consumption patterns, including related shifts in lifestyles and diets in some countries, contrasted with growing pockets of poverty in other countries, can further stress the natural resource base and the ability of Governments to satisfy increasing demands. This is compounded by water scarcity, soil and land degradation, growing pollution of streams, and climate change. The situation is further complicated by the ongoing conflicts and security conditions that plague the region and undermine the ability to manage the sustainability of natural resources. The management of natural resources in areas that are under occupation is a unique complex parameter that also must be considered.

Constructing an analytical framework for examining the WEF security nexus for application in the Arab region thus requires a joint vision based on common principles that can be accepted by all Arab countries. This can be achieved by promoting a people-centered approach that is grounded in the SDGs that define the 2030 Sustainable Development Agenda at the global and regional levels.

A people-centred approach to development that is guided by universal human rights principles regarding the right to water, food and development can provide the basis upon which a nexus analytical framework can be constructed in the Arab region. Such an approach considers the three main components of the WEF security nexus as equally important. Therefore, the proposed human rights-based approach does not discriminate between water, energy and food as human rights and aims to achieve universal access to these three components over the long term. This is different from the WEF security nexus approaches proposed by SEI and the World Economic Forum in 2011, which prioritized water resources above the other components of the nexus. As such, a universal approach to the WEF security nexus for the Arab region would be consistent with global, regional and national development goals.

Applying such a nexus in the context of the Arab region can also benefit from specificities that are evident when examining smaller scales of analysis at the regional, national and subnational levels. Such an approach allows for the incorporation of lessons learned from the application of IWRM tools for improved water security, regional efforts to support SE4All for improved energy security, and investments aimed at promoting sustainable agricultural practices. It also allows more reliable trade regimes for improved food security within the context of climate change and the need to ensure WEF security for all.

The elaboration of this nexus approach needs to consider the environment in which nexus analytical frameworks will be applied in the Arab region in the decades to come. This requires consideration of climate change, in particular the way in which climate change will affect the ability to achieve WEF security in the region. For the Arab region, however, climate change is considered a driver that affects WEF security and is not a goal itself.

Such an analytical framework for pursuing the WEF security nexus in the Arab region and within the context of the 2030 Development Agenda is illustrated in figure 10.

At the operational level, it should also consider the scale and scope of analysis, existing institutional and policy frameworks, and the ways in which technology can improve the ability to achieve WEF security in an integrated manner in order to progress towards sustainable development.

Figure 10. The water-energy-food security nexus

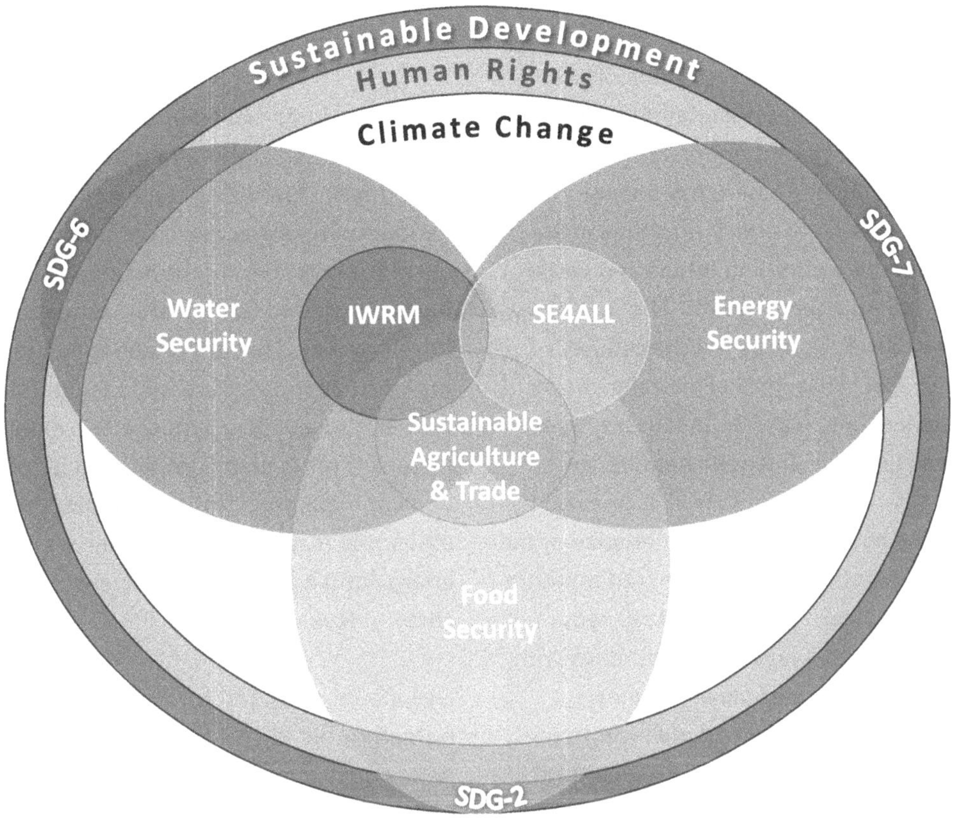

Source: Authors.

Note: SDG stands for Sustainable Development Goal; IWRM for integrated water resources management; and SE4All for Sustainable Energy for All.

1. Scale and scope of analysis

The present report largely focuses on the regional scale of analysis for examining the nexus, particularly the opportunity to foster cross-sectoral dialogue and integrated planning among Arab States. This point of view is used to examine how the nexus can foster collective action through regional priority setting, positioning, negotiations, and supportive action at the national level. Arab States will also benefit from the nexus as an analytical framework for improved coordination of policies and strategies for the integrated management of natural resources, especially in areas where resources are shared or where the disparity in natural endowments across countries is a factor influencing the achievement of regional specified goals.

Regional level analysis in this report encompasses any inter-State approach aimed at considering the WEF security nexus within or between geopolitical regions, across national boundaries or within shared water basins. When applied at the basin level, the scale of analysis can be considered similar to the approach put forth by ICIMOD, ECE and UNEP within a water-energy-food-ecosystem approach to the nexus.

For instance, the WEF security nexus offers potential for improving understanding, dialogue and sustainable development planning at the basin level by allowing riparian States to examine cross-sectoral policy priorities in a shared basin when pursuing integrated water resources management (IWRM). The Inventory of Shared Water Resources in Western Asia prepared by ESCWA and the Federal Institute for Geosciences and Natural Resources (BGR) takes a nexus approach when characterizing transboundary water resources.[33] It does so by reviewing the hydrological characteristics of the nine shared river basins and 22 shared aquifers located in the eastern part of the Arab region. It then elaborates basin-level characteristics with regard to population, climate and water development and the uses of water within the basin, including hydropower and agricultural development. This information can provide a baseline for informing cross-sectoral dialogue among riparian States as negotiations at the basin level do not only involve managers of water resources but also ministries of foreign affairs, planning and agriculture, among others. A nexus analytical framework can thus build upon an integrated approach to the management of water resources by allowing countries to highlight their different socioeconomic and environmental priorities both within and outside the water box in view to optimizing WEF security at the national and basins levels. Similar benefits can be found when examining transboundary ecosystems, such as wetlands and bioreserves that provide benefits for water, energy, agriculture, and environment, and eventually human welfare.

2. Institutional and policy framework

A human rights-based approach to development and the human rights obligations contained in the different United Nations conventions ratified by member parties place the onus on Governments to fulfil, protect and respect the human rights to food, water, sanitation, and development. This is a challenge in the Arab region as resources are increasingly scarce and further stressed by domestic and external factors. This is also complicated by overlapping and conflicting institutional mandates between ministries responsible for water resources, energy and agriculture at the sectoral and cross-sectoral levels.

Despite these institutional complications, a human rights-based approach is consistent with policy goals aimed at ensuring WEF security, which are shared by all ministries and Government agencies at country level. The differences lie in each institution's approach in achieving these aims. A nexus conceptual framework can thus assist in setting common principles that must be satisfied when seeking to find a balance between resources and needs across the three sectors.

The Arab Charter on Human Rights entered into force in 2008 after its ratification by the seventh member of the League of Arab States.[34] This Charter has been ratified by 13 countries in total, namely, Algeria, Bahrain, Jordan, Kuwait, Lebanon, Libya, Palestine, Qatar, Saudi Arabia, the Sudan, Syrian Arab Republic, United Arab

Emirates and Yemen, and more recently Iraq. The Charter refers to the rights to water and food specifically in the following two articles:

- Article 38: "Every person has the right to an adequate standard of living for himself and his family, which ensures their well-being and a decent life, including food, clothing, housing, services and the right to a healthy environment. The State Parties shall take the necessary measures commensurate with their resources to guarantee these rights;"[35]
- Article 39 in parts 2.e and 2.f: "The measures taken by States shall include the following: Provision of basic nutrition and safe drinking water for all" and "Combating environmental pollution and providing proper sanitation systems".[36]

The institutional and policy framework for operationalizing the WEF security is also available in the Arab Region, which needs to function within the context of existing Arab strategies and action plans.[37] Several strategies and action plans exist that can support the nexus approach.

(a) Arab water security strategy

In 2011, the Arab Ministerial Water Council (AMWC) of the League of Arab States adopted the Arab Strategy for Water Security in the Arab Region to Meet the Challenges and Future Needs for Sustainable Development 2010-2030.[38] The main goal is to meet the sustainable development challenges by means of a work plan that tackles several aspects of water resources management, such as capacity building, research and development, provision

for drinking and irrigation water services, unconventional water resources, and IWRM. The strategy is meant to unify and guide Arab efforts in managing their water resources, and was operationalized in an action plan approved by the AMWC in May 2014. Although this strategy does not elaborate a nexus paradigm, it refers to the importance of considering the three components of the WEF security nexus with respect to one another as a means to overcome water shortages in the Arab region.

(b) Arab food security strategy

The agriculture sector and related food security have been addressed by the League of Arab States through several declarations, policies and strategies. The 2004 Tunis Summit Declaration addressed sustainable agricultural development and food security in the Arab region through a call for coordination between country specific agriculture policies within a regional Arab agricultural development strategy. This was followed by the Riyadh Arab Summit resolutions in 2007 that approved the Strategy for Sustainable Arab Agricultural Development for the Upcoming Two Decades (2005-2025),[39] which was adopted by the ministers of agriculture in the Arab region with the support of the Arab Organization for Agricultural Development (AOAD).

The strategy's main objective is agriculture development characterized by effective resource utilization capable of achieving food security while securing sustainable livelihoods in the agricultural sector. Furthermore, the Arab Economic and Social Development Summit held in Kuwait in 2009 endorsed the Arab Food

Security Emergency Programme, which aims at increasing and stabilizing food production in the Arab region. It focuses on improving efficient use of available water resources, strengthening the research and transfer of advanced agricultural technology, improving agricultural investment, and developing farmers' institutional frameworks. An underlying driver for these strategies is the understated water scarcity in the region combined with the lack of suitable agricultural land.

(c) Arab renewable energy strategy

The third Arab Economic and Social Development Summit in Riyadh in January 2013 approved and ratified the Pan-Arab Strategy for the Development of Renewable Energy Applications: 2010-2030,[40] which provides a roadmap for the development of renewable energy in the Arab region over a twenty year period.

This renewable energy strategy sets the target of expanding installed power generation capacity in the region to approximately 75 gigawatt (GW) by 2030.[41] It aims to maximize the utilization of abundant renewable energy, the diversification of energy sources to improve energy security, availing the required energy resources and services necessary to support development, improving longevity of regional oil and gas reserves, and reducing the environmental impacts associated with traditional oil and gas usage. The intersectoral linkages of this strategy are inherent in the cross-cutting horizontal and vertical effects that are fully exposed within a nexus framework.

(d) National level

The institutional framework for applying the WEF security nexus at the national scale is more advanced than at the regional scale, with many Arab countries already having combined ministries whose mandate covers two or more components of the nexus. For example, combined ministries for water and electricity/energy exist in Bahrain, Kuwait, Lebanon, Morocco, Qatar, Saudi Arabia, and the Sudan. Water and irrigation/agriculture ministries exist in Egypt, Jordan and Tunisia.

However, institutional setup alone is insufficient if these institutions fail to have the proper mechanism or mandate for cross-sectoral integrated planning. Indeed, operationalizing a nexus approach in the Arab region will prove challenging since the region is characterized by a silo mentality with sector-focused governance structures, sector strategies and policies, and budgetary plans that are organized in accordance with line ministries. Therefore, institutional frameworks will need to be flexible and dynamic, and politically committed to pursue cross-sectoral dialogue and integrated approaches to policy formulation and implementation.

3. Technology and efficiency

Local research and innovations for the transfer and development of appropriate technologies need to respond to regional conditions and local specificities. In doing so, Arab States can benefit from and adapt new and emerging technologies to improve water use and energy efficiency, agricultural productivity, and the adoption of new renewable energy technologies. However, doing so requires investment and financing as well as mechanisms to encourage innovation, adaptation, and research and development in the region.

As in the global context, technology decisions should not be made on the basis of maximizing efficiency alone. Economic efficiency evaluations outside a WEF security nexus framework may backfire and lead to unintended consequences if not appropriately designed. For example, the efforts of the Government of Saudi Arabia during the 1980s to promote wheat cultivation to enhance food security through national food self-sufficiency policies were reconsidered in the 1990s in order to reduce the impact wheat cultivation was having on its non-renewable groundwater resource reserves. However, while the most economically efficient mechanism for pursuing this policy change was to cut fixed wheat commodity prices and reduce associated subsidies related to wheat production, the effect was that farmers switched to fodder production, which has even higher water requirements.

As another example, many agricultural cooperatives and farmers in the Arab region are investing in modern, energy-efficient solar water pumping technologies in order to reduce energy costs. Such technologies are also considered an effective mitigation of climate change as heavily polluting diesel generators are no longer needed. Consequently, the production and sales of these new efficient pumps have proliferated throughout the region and are generally considered a sustainable green business. However, this has encouraged greater groundwater extraction and threatens

water security in the very near term as the cost of energy is no longer a limiting factor. This poses a significant challenge to water resources management, namely to find ways to monitor and regulate water extraction by these efficient, modular pumping units.

Furthermore, a people-centred approach to the WEF security nexus may make efforts to achieve WEF security counterproductive to programmes and projects that aim to maximize efficiency in natural resource use. Technology choices must thus be made within a regional context that considers the current security conditions and associated constraints based on universal human rights principles. Doing so may require political decisions that do not seek the most resource-efficient option. For instance, arguments seeking to maximize economic efficiency may claim that arid Arab countries would benefit from becoming fully dependent on food imports from more water-rich countries; however, such arguments to do not take into consideration the security aspects associated with ensuring water, energy and food for all.

4. Regional approaches and initiatives for operationalizing the nexus

Regional-level dialogue on the nexus has been fostered for the past five years. ESCWA, the League of Arab States and their associated intergovernmental bodies, in collaboration with the German Society for International Cooperation (Deutsche Gesellschaft für Internationale Zusammenarbeit (GIZ) GmbH), the Swedish International Development Cooperation Agency (Sida) and other international partners have laid the foundation for fostering regional cooperation regarding the nexus across borders and sectors.

This has largely been achieved through the introduction of nexus concepts in intergovernmental committee meetings and sessions, stakeholder consultations and the launching of regional projects and initiatives.

(a) Prioritizing consideration of issues regarding the nexus

At the intergovernmental level, members of the ESCWA Committee on Water Resources and the ESCWA Committee on Energy met in Beirut in June 2012 to identify a set of priorities for consideration and action in order to increase understanding of nexus-related approaches in the Arab region. The purpose of the meeting was to initiate intersectoral dialogue and exchange between water and energy officials at the national and regional levels. Preparations for the meeting included the completion of a joint questionnaire by the members of both committees, followed by an interactive discussion on the areas of work they wanted to address on the water-energy nexus. This resulted in the members of both committees collectively identifying the following seven water-energy nexus priority areas for examination:[42]

- Raising awareness and dissemination knowledge;
- Improving the harmonization of public policies;
- Examining the link between water security and energy security;
- Improving efficiency;
- Increasing knowledge of technological choices;
- Promoting renewable energy;
- Integrating climate change and natural disasters factors in decision making.

These recommendations were subsequently endorsed at the tenth session of the ESCWA Committee on Water Resources and at the ninth session of the ESCWA Committee on Energy. Capacity-building on these priority areas is thus being organized for the Arab States and the members of the above-mentioned two intergovernmental committees by ESCWA, with funding provided by the United Nations Development Account (see below).

(b) Arab Initiative on the Water, Energy and Food Nexus

The League of Arab States is exploring ways for the WEF nexus to support Arab member States. The League of Arab States and GIZ thus organized a WEF nexus dialogue during the Regional South-South Arab Development Expo in Doha in February 2014. The dialogue outlined components of a regional initiative on the nexus aimed at engaging members of the AMWC, Arab Ministerial Council on Electricity (AMCE), and Council of Arab Ministers Responsible for the Environment (CAMRE), noting that CAMRE has been largely responsible for regional follow-up related to Rio+20, the United Nations Conference on Sustainable Development held in Rio de Janeiro in 2012, and the SDGs.

The effort led to the adoption of resolutions by the AMWC and AMCE that invite the League of Arab States, GIZ and ESCWA to solicit funding to implement nexus-related activities and studies, and to organize meetings for Arab experts on nexus-related priorities, in support of the finalized Arab Initiative on the Water, Energy and Food Nexus.

In connection with this Initiative, the League of Arab States and ESCWA convened an Expert Group Meeting on the Water, Energy and Food Security Nexus in the Arab Region in Amman in March 2015. The purpose of the meeting was to advance understanding of the WEF security nexus and encourage discussions on how a nexus framework may be used to improve integrated natural resources management and aid in achieving progress towards sustainable development in the region. The meeting was held back-to-back with the tenth session of the ESCWA Committee on Energy and the eleventh session of the ESCWA Committee on Water Resources. The meetings resulted in a series of conclusions related to the nexus and its ability to support the achievement of sustainable development and the need to support further work in the Arab region through an inclusive approach taking into consideration institutional and policy issues and national and regional specificities.[43]

The initiative is being further supported by a project launched by GIZ together with the Arabian Gulf University in 2015 in order to prepare five policy briefs on the WEF nexus. The briefs will address the political economy of the nexus, the institutional landscape, integrated planning and implementation mechanisms, green economy and sustainable development, and nexus capacity development in the Arab region.

(c) Building capacity on the water-energy nexus in the region

ESCWA is addressing the recommendations of member countries and identified priorities through various activities, including a United Nations Development Account project aimed at building the capacity of ESCWA member countries in the water-energy nexus for achieving sustainable development goals. Launched in January 2015, this project is being implemented along two parallel tracks. One track is aimed at senior Government officials responsible for the formulation of policies and strategies, while the other targets technical staff of ministries who are more involved in the operational aspects of water and energy resources management, and the delivery of water- and energy-related services. A regional policy toolkit targeted at the senior Government officials will be developed for each of the seven identified priorities, complimented by three technical toolkits covering resource efficiency, technology transfer and renewable energy. Knowledge transfer and exchange of experience will be strengthened by several regional workshops and demand-driven pilot projects.

(d) Building capacity on the food-water nexus in the region

ESCWA launched a second project focused on the nexus entitled Promoting Food and Water Security through Cooperation and Capacity Development in the Arab Region in December 2014 with funding provided by Sida. The project is led by ESCWA and implemented in consultation with the League of Arab States and its associated ministerial councils and specialized agencies responsible for water, agricultural and food security, and other regional organizations serving the Arab region. The project aims at strengthening the intersectoral dialogue across water and agriculture institutions and to build capacity in order to assess the impacts of changing water availability on agricultural production in the

Arab region in view of climate change. The project also aims to enhance capacity for coordinated regional policy development on food and water security and to enhance the capacity of the region to assess the status of food security and improve the efficiency of agricultural and food production systems in the Arab region.

Although each of the above projects directly deals with binary relations of water-energy or food-water only, they complement each other in addressing the three pillars of the WEF security nexus. This approach is currently better suited for the actual institutional setup of most ministries in the Arab region, which are usually mandated with the management of two sectors at the most. These initiatives will help broaden the thinking beyond the current silo mentality and act as stepping stones for more complex nexus approaches in the future.

II. The Nexus from a Shared-Basin Perspective

The management of shared water resources becomes even more complex when considering the relationship between water, energy and food security as the system in which the nexus is framed. Most prominent are interative inter-State relationships and the likelihood of differences in development priorities between upstream and downstream riparian countries. Grounding the nexus in a human rights approach within the context of shared water basins can facilitate the prioritization process during which a balance needs to be found and trade-offs need to be considered between water, energy and food security aims in view of complexities related to geopolitics, sovereignty and security within a shared basin. This chapter illustrates the importance of considering the WEF security nexus when pursuing cooperation with regard to shared water resources in the Arab region as a means to support the achievement of common goals. Two shared surface water basins, the Euphrates river basin and the Nile river basin, and two shared groundwater basins, the Saq-Ram Aquifer System (West), which is often called the Disi Aquifer, and the North-Western Sahara Aquifer System (NWSAS), are examined in order to identify how a nexus perspective can further cross-sectoral understanding of shared water resources with a view to ensuring WEF security for all.

A. Overview

The Arab region is one of the most arid regions in the world, with 66 per cent of its freshwater resources crossing the boundaries of one country or more.[44] This makes achieving water security in particular and sustainable development in general especially challenging. The situation is even more complicated for water basins that are shared between Arab and non-Arab countries or for those which are situated on or below occupied land, such as parts of the Jordan River basin. Historically, cities, agriculture, commerce, and industry have thrived along shared surface water resources in the region. Advances in drilling and pumping technologies have produced opportunities to access shared groundwater resources in more remote geographical regions in order to meet growing demand. The importance of effectively managing shared surface water and groundwater resources is increasing as economic demands and environmental pressures contribute to increasing water scarcity. The dependency of Arab States on external water resources increases the need for better cooperation between riparian States as the management of a shared water resource in one country may have significant effects on the ability of other countries sharing the same resource to benefit from it.

In the Arab region, there are 27 shared surface water basins: 14 out of the 22 Arab countries are riparian States.[45, 46] There are over 270 dams of various capacities and uses situated within these basins.[47] Some of these dams are entirely dedicated to or at least include a component for hydropower generation, while many are used for storage and irrigation as shown in map 1. The management of these shared surface water resources and the alteration of their natural river flows have allowed for the development of large irrigation projects, hydropower generation and the storage of reserves. However, quantity, quality and seasonality of these flows for different purposes must be considered across riparian States in order to avoid potential negative impacts that upstream management schemes could have on downstream users.

Map 1. Shared surface water basins, surface water irrigated areas and dams with hydropower generation in the Arab region

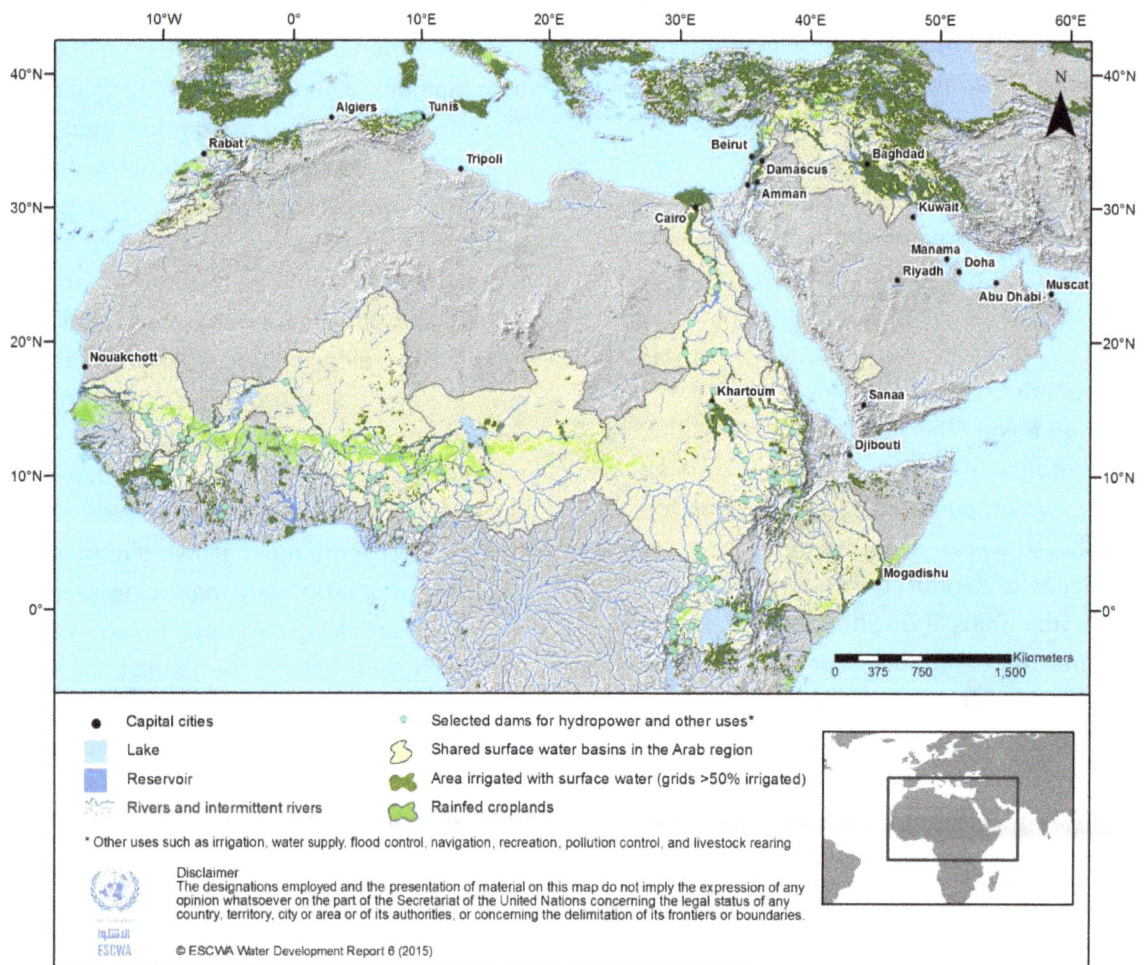

Sources: Extracted from ESCWA and BGR, 2013a; FAO, 2006; GlobCover Database, FAO, 2013b.

Map 2. Shared groundwater basins and groundwater irrigated areas in the Arab region

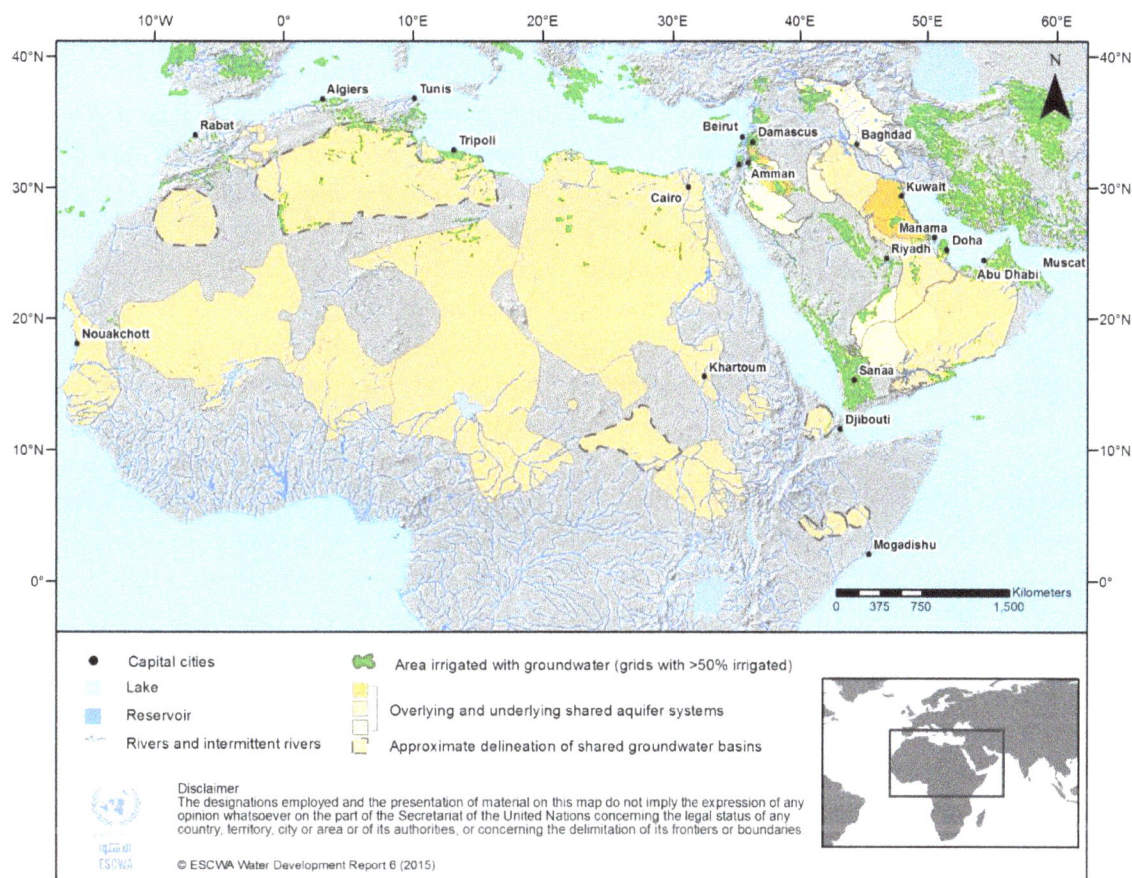

Sources: Extracted from ESCWA and BGR, 2013a; IGRAC, 2015; FAO, 2013b.

The number of shared groundwater resources in the Arab region outnumbers that of shared surface water basins: there are 40 shared aquifers in 21 out of 22 Arab countries.[48, 49] Shared groundwater basins cover almost 58 per cent of the region in terms of area and are used to support large-scale irrigation projects as illustrated in map 2. The extent of shared groundwater aquifers and the advancement of pumping technologies have prompted reliance on these resources by the agriculture sector and Governments in their pursuit of food self-sufficiency, despite the fact that large volumes of groundwater come from so-called fossil groundwater reserves and are thus non-renewable. This puts decision-makers in a dilemma regarding the use of these groundwater reserves and ensuring water and food security for present and future generations.

Groundwater abstraction is also an energy-intensive practice that has been subsidized for many decades by many Arab countries, which has led to the overabstraction of groundwater resources. The mining of fossil groundwater reserves lowers the groundwater table and renders deeper groundwater reserves economically inaccessible to small-scale farmers, increasing the dominance of large-scale agricultural companies. In middle- and low-income countries, the depletion of groundwater reserves has fuelled the migration of small-scale farmers, particularly men, to primary and secondary urban cities in search of employment. Consequently, this development has changed the character of rural communities and increased the number of women heading households, while also generating socioeconomic pressures, exacerbating prevailing inequalities and fostering discontent in urban centres.

Climate change and climate variability will increase the region's dependency on shared surface and groundwater resources. The nexus analytical framework could serve as a useful tool to better assist Arab countries in exploring the concrete interlinkages between WEF sectors in shared water basins. The following sections provide case studies on shared surface and groundwater resources, focusing on WEF nexus interlinkages and opportunities for better cooperation over resources using a nexus framework. However, a key to cooperation in the region is the respect of historical water use rights and the understanding of water as a human right.

B. Euphrates river basin

1. Mapping of water, energy and food/agricultural water use along the Euphrates river

The Euphrates river, as it flows from its source to the Shatt el Arab, is shared by three riparian countries, namely, Turkey, the Syrian Arab Republic and Iraq, while the catchment of the Euphrates river basin also encompasses smaller areas in Jordan and Saudi Arabia. The Euphrates basin area covers nearly 440,000 km2 distributed between Iraq (47 per cent), Turkey (28 per cent), the Syrian Arab Republic (22 per cent), Saudi Arabia (2.97 per cent), and Jordan (0.03 per cent).[50] The river originates in the mountains of eastern Turkey and flows south where it crosses into the Syrian Arab Republic at the town of Jarablus. In the Syrian Arab Republic, three tributaries join the Euphrates before it leaves the Syrian Arab Republic at Al Bukamal and enters Iraq. The Euphrates river is joined downstream by the Tigris river to form the Shatt al Arab that discharges into the Persian Gulf near Kuwait, as shown in map 3. A population of nearly 23 million resided within the basin in 2012 prior to the more recent armed conflicts in Iraq and the Syrian Arab Republic. The pre-conflict population distribution within the basin was estimated to be 10.2 million people in Iraq, 7.15 million in Turkey,and 5.69 million in the Syrian Arab Republic,[51] noting that numerous cities and communities situated outside the Euphrates river basin have been served by the river's flows, such as the Syrian city of Aleppo.

Nearly 89 per cent of the total Euphrates flow regime is generated from Turkey. The Syrian Arab Republic contributes approximately 11 per cent of the total flow while contribution from Iraq is negligible.[52] The pre-1973 mean annual discharge at the Syrian-Turkish border was approximately 30 BCM, which has decreased to 22.8 BCM since 1990 mainly due to climate change and the construction of large dams in Turkey as part of the Southeastern Anatolia Project (GAP).[53] The volume of the river's natural flow is exceeded four to five times by the maximum storage capacity of all dams and reservoirs on the river. Thus, with the onset of several large dams, the flow has not only decreased but has become highly regulated, especially in the runoff generating area in Turkey. Since the construction of these dams, high flow discharge water from March to July is stored to be later released in the low-flow period of September to October when most needed for winter crops.

Although the regulation of the river may have had some positive effects, the lower flows had dire consequences on the quality of the water. One of the major water quality challenges facing the Euphrates basin is water salinity. River salinity increases as the river water flows from the Syrian-Turkish border towards Iraq due to the gypsiferous nature of the soils in the Syrian Arab Republic. The salinity problem increases dramatically in Iraq due to the reduced flow, high rates of evaporation, intensive agriculture activities and irrigation drains. In some parts, the water salinity reaches high levels making it unsuitable for both domestic and agricultural uses. The salinity problem is a chronic problem for Iraq and led the country to construct the Third River or Main Outfall Drain. The artificial canal, which extends from Baghdad to the Gulf, is used for irrigation drainage from land between the Euphrates and Tigris rivers. The main objective of the canal was to protect the Euphrates from the saline water of the irrigation drainage. Other effects of the reduced flows include the shrinking of the Southern Iraqi marshlands where only 10 per cent remain functioning and the demise of the sea coastal marine ecosystem due to increased salinity.[54] In order to avoid water shortages resulting from reduced flows, Iraq built a canal to divert the Tigris river water to the Euphrates river.[55] This has indirectly affected the Tigris River

in terms of quantity of water available in the basin and increasing problems with salinity.

The Euphrates not only supports the residing population in terms of domestic use, forming the corner stone of the national water balance in the Syrian Arab Republic and Iraq and to a lesser extent in Turkey, but also supports considerable agricultural activities and hydro-power generation from several dams in all three riparian countries, as seen in map 3. The Euphrates in this sense lends itself to examination through a WEF security nexus analytical framework.

The estimated irrigated area in the basin is approximately 2.3 million hectare (ha); the agricultural share of water use is nearly 70 per cent.[56] Turkey currently irrigates approximately 230,000 ha of land in the Euphrates basin with ultimate plans as part of the Southeastern Anatolia Project (GAP) to expand this to 1.8 million ha,[57] irrigated from both the Euphrates and Tigris. Prior to the current conflict, the Syrian Arab Republic mainly used the basin water resources for large irrigation projects ranging between 325,000 ha in 2000 to 270,000 ha in 2010 with a further 325,000 ha earmarked for future development.[58] Iraq had been utilizing the water of the Euphrates prior to any development plans by Turkey or the Syrian Arab Republic; already in the 1960s, it had 1.2 million ha of irrigated land. Current estimates of irrigated land in Iraq varies between 1 and 1.5 million ha with an estimated total potential of irrigable land within the Iraqi share of the Euphrates varying between 1.8 million and 4 million ha.[59] This highlights the importance of the Euphrates river basin as regards the food security of the riparian countries, mainly the Syrian Arab Republic and Iraq, and the effect of the armed conflict on the basin.

Map 3. The Euphrates river basin with major dams and irrigated areas

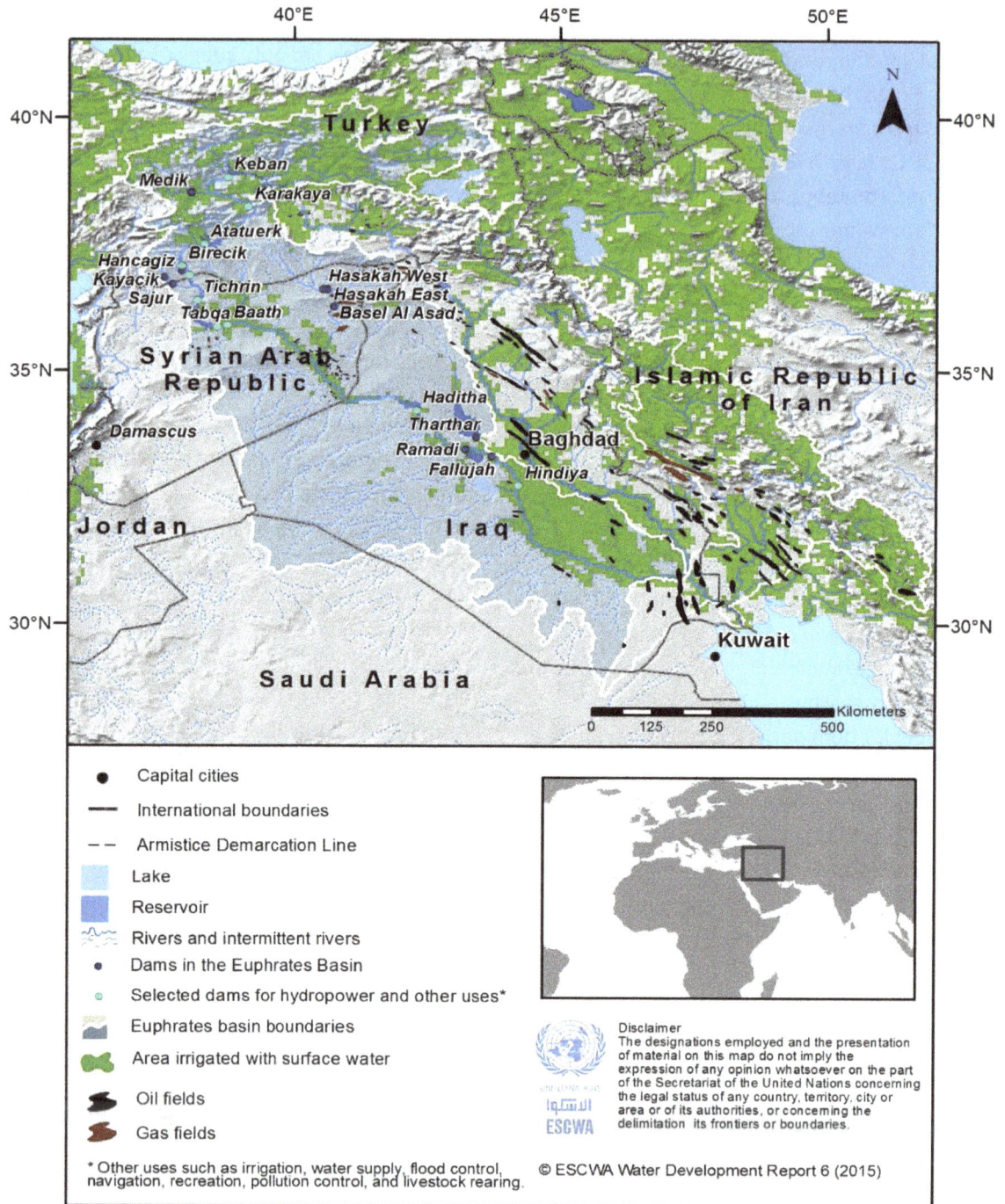

Legend:
- Capital cities
- International boundaries
- Armistice Demarcation Line
- Lake
- Reservoir
- Rivers and intermittent rivers
- Dams in the Euphrates Basin
- Selected dams for hydropower and other uses*
- Euphrates basin boundaries
- Area irrigated with surface water
- Oil fields
- Gas fields

* Other uses such as irrigation, water supply, flood control, navigation, recreation, pollution control, and livestock rearing.

© ESCWA Water Development Report 6 (2015)

Disclaimer
The designations employed and the presentation of material on this map do not imply the expression of any opinion whatsoever on the part of the Secretariat of the United Nations concerning the legal status of any country, territory, city or area or of its authorities, or concerning the delimitation its frontiers or boundaries.

ESCWA

Sources: Extracted from ESCWA and BGR, 2013; FAO, 2013b; Christian, 2000; WorldMap, 2011.

In terms of energy, there are two components to consider: hydropower generation and the water dependency of oil fields. In terms of hydropower, all three riparian countries have erected dams on the Euphrates that are either dedicated to hydropower generation or include a component for (map 3).

The total estimated installed hydropower capacity is approximately 8,580 megawatt (MW), with Turkey ranking first among the three countries at 6,391 MW, followed by the Syrian Arab Republic at 1,529 MW, and Iraq at 660 MW.[60] These figures fail to take into account future plans to expand the hydropower capacity through the completion of the GAP in Turkey or other projects. As regards oil production, the water requirement varies from one field to another and with maturity; it is reported that the Euphrates Company in the Syrian Arab Republic requires one barrel of fresh water together with five barrels of recycled water from the Euphrates for each barrel of oil.[61]

2. Impact of conflict on water, energy and food security along the Euphrates river

Although bilateral agreements, treaties and protocols regarding the Euphrates basin date as far back as the 1920s, there is, at present, no basin-wide agreement or institutional structure that involves the three riparian countries. Historically, the norm regarding the Euphrates basin has been unilateral development plans and dams, which has increased tension. The only trilateral form of cooperation was through a joint technical committee that had started as a bilateral committee between Iraq and Turkey in 1980 and was joined by the Syrian Arab Republic in 1983.[62] The committee's work

focused on the exchange of data, sharing information on the construction of dams and irrigation schemes, but deadlock led to its dissolution in 1993.[63]

The 1997 United Nations Convention on the Law of Non-navigational Use of International Watercourses may not serve as a proper tool for the management of the Euphrates as Turkey voted against it. A point of contention between the riparian countries is the consideration of the Euphrates and Tigris as one or two basins. Turkey prefers to consider the two basins as one single basin for the allocation of water among the riparian countries, while Iraq and the Syrian Arab Republic prefer to consider them as two separate basins with water allocations negotiated separately.[64]

The allocation of water in the Euphrates basin is governed by two bilateral agreements: the 1987 Protocol on Economic Cooperation between the Syrian Arab Republic and Turkey that guarantees a yearly average release of 16 billion cubic metres (BCM) from the Euphrates at the Syrian-Turkish border; and a water-sharing agreement established in 1990 between Iraq and the Syrian Arab Republic that allocates 42 per cent of the Euphrates water measured at the Syrian-Turkish border to the Syrian Arab Republic and 58 per cent to Iraq.[65]

The relationships between the riparian countries had improved in the early 2000s, but this has changed again with the most recent drought that started in 2006 and the eruption of the Syrian crisis in 2011. However, both the Syrian Arab Republic and Turkey have since reaffirmed their commitment to the signed bilateral agreement on sharing the Euphrates water.

The current armed conflicts in the Syrian Arab Republic and in Iraq have greatly affected the management of the Euphrates. Monitoring records of the Syrian parts of the river have been lost; proper maintenance and management of hydraulic structures are nearly non-existent; and different armed groups control a number of hydraulic structures, and thus a considerable share of the Euphrates water.

The limited control of the flow regime from several dams has affected WEF security. Cities such as Aleppo that depend on the Euphrates for domestic water supply are under water stress, and hydropower generation has been severely affected. Agriculture activity that has been severely hampered by consecutive years of drought prior to the conflict is further affected by the uncontrolled water flows caused by armed conflict. Some academic studies even proposed that drought, water and food insecurity and climate change may have contributed to the instability of the region.[66]

The Syrian crisis has forced four million people to flee the country and another 7.6 million have sought refuge internally.[67] In Iraq, 1.9 million Iraqis or 5.7 per cent of the population suffer from food deprivation,[68] and a further 4 million Iraqis or 14 per cent of the population are vulnerable to food insecurity.[69] This displacement of civilians has also redistributed the demand for the Euphrates' water resources, specifically in Turkey, which is hosting a large refugee population, and in the Syrian Arab Republic, where agricultural activities and food security are greatly affected.

3. Implications of inter-State cooperation for sustainable development within a water-energy-food nexus perspective under conflict conditions

In particular in areas of armed conflict in Iraq and the Syrian Arab Republic, transboundary cooperation for the management of the Euphrates basin is challenging and any development will not be a priority especially in. In order to minimize the humanitarian crisis related to the WEF security nexus, current efforts should be focused on maintaining the Euphrates' minimum flow regimes that were previously agreed upon. Meanwhile, the WEF nexus analytical framework could be used to initiate an academic technical discussion group made up by members from the three riparian countries. The focus would be on the Euphrates basin and on finding answers to many of the unresolved questions about the river's hydrology, the development of a future unified flow regime and meteorological monitoring network, climate change impacts on the river basin, future water storage options, and the allocation of water between agriculture and hydropower. This expert group would help develop a mutual understanding of the current challenges and would enhance dialogue between the different parties. However, in areas of armed conflict in Iraq and the Syrian Arab Republic, transboundary cooperation for the management of the Euphrates basin constitutes a challenge and any development is currently not given the necessary priority.

The WEF security nexus may provide a future incentive for better cooperation and sharing where a water-focused approach has failed to provide a basin-wide agreement. Several reasons are behind this failure, including mistrust between the riparian States stemming from a series of unilateral water development projects; and lack of incentive to reach an agreement on shared water resources as river flow is mostly generated in one country.

There are many entry points under the WEF nexus for cooperation between the three riparian countries; hydropower is one of them. Currently, Iraq and the Syrian Arab Republic are suffering from a huge shortage in electricity supply. In response thereto, Iraq is planning for a number of additional dams and hydropower stations. Carrying forward such plans will mean huge costs for the country and further water losses due to the high evaporation rates in a country already suffering from water shortage, not to mention the potential lost socioeconomic opportunity caused by diverting water from agriculture purposes to the generation of hydropower.[70] Turkey is losing a great share of the electrical power generated by the Euphrates basin hydropower plants. This is the case because electrical demand is concentrated in the west of the country while hydropower stations are located in the east, resulting in electrical power being transmitted over long distances through inefficient transmission networks. Such losses and costs can be minimized dramatically by exporting the electrical power generated along the Euphrates to closer regions in the Syrian Arab Republic and Iraq. Additionally, Turkey can benefit from preferable oil and gas prices offered by Iraq and the Syrian Arab Republic to support this cooperative arrangement. This might have great impact on the river flow regime as Turkey would be encouraged to release more water through its hydropower stations, largely benefitting the

agriculture sector in the Syrian Arab Republic and Iraq.

Another entry point is the idea to store water in Turkey's dams. The country has a massive storing capacity with evaporation rates far lower than those in Iraq and the Syrian Arab Republic. This means that both countries reserve their right over their shares but can release them when needed the most. Turkey can charge a storage tariff to cover management and operational costs. The Syrian Arab Republic and Turkey save the costs and risks involved in the construction of additional dams, reduce the environmental impacts and save water lost to evaporation. Even though the WEF security nexus may have been a factor triggering the crisis currently facing the region, it can be evolved into a main tool for future negotiations and allow an improved regional management of the resources across the Euphrates basin compared to the current suboptimal management at the country level, thereby creating win-win situations for all riparian States.

C. Nile river basin

1. Mapping of water, energy and food/agricultural water uses along the Nile river

Eleven countries, namely, Burundi, Democratic Republic of Congo, Egypt, Eritrea, Ethiopia, Kenya, Rwanda, South Sudan, the Sudan, Tanzania, and Uganda, share the Nile river, which has a length of 6.695 km and a catchment area of 3.1 million km^2,[71] as illustrated in map 4. Approximately 238 million people reside within the Nile basin area, with Egypt having the largest population residing within the basin and the Democratic Republic of Congo the smallest.[72] The importance of the Nile to the downstream countries is made apparent by the high concentration of population along the Nile in Egypt and the Sudan, while further upstream the population concentration follows areas of high rainfall.[73] The population of the Nile basin countries is projected to increase by 53 per cent by the year 2030,[74] increasing the pressure on the Nile basin and the demand for water, food and energy.

Map 4. The Nile river basin with surface water irrigated areas and major hydropower dams

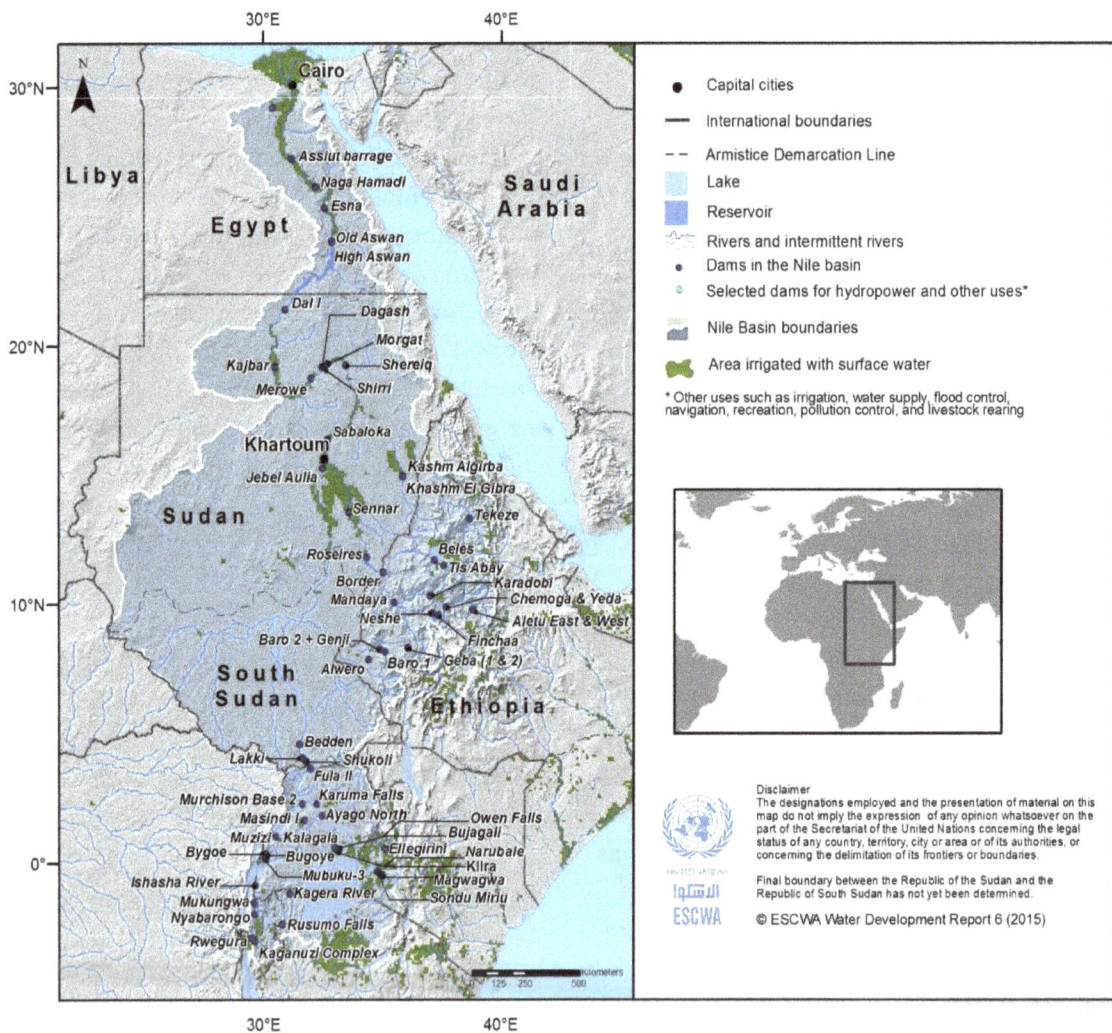

Sources: Extracted from FAO, 2013b; and FAO, 2006.

The estimated water flow of the Nile at Aswan in Egypt is 84.5 km³/year, with most of this flow generated in only 15 per cent of the basin area,[75] while the remaining areas are semi-arid to arid with high evapotranspiration rates. The Nile flow only constitutes approximately 5 per cent of the total rainfall in the basin of 1660 km³/year.[76] In fact, rainfall across the basin is highly variable, with the highlands of the south and east receiving more than 2000 mm while lowlands in the north receive less than 10 mm as is the case for much of Egypt.[77] Prior to the 1970s, variability and seasonality of rainfall were regulated by a series of dams along the subsidiary rivers of the Nile, mainly for irrigation purposes in Egypt and the Sudan.[78] The Aswan High Dam with a total storage of nearly twice the annual flow was constructed in 1970 to guarantee flows to Egypt.[79]

The agriculture sector is the major consumer of water in the Nile basin, with a 78 per cent consumption of the peak water volume.[80] The total irrigated area in the basin is approximately 5.5 million ha, with almost 99 per cent located in Egypt (60 per cent) and the Sudan (39 per cent), and the remaining area distributed across the upper riparian countries. The upper riparian countries' agriculture sector is predominantly rain-fed, covering a total rain-fed area of 33 million hectares. The Sudan has the largest rain-fed area among all Nile riparian States, followed by Uganda, Ethiopia, Tanzania, Kenya, Rwanda, Burundi, and Eretria, with livestock being an integral constituent of the agricultural sector.[81] Southern Sudan also has rain-fed agriculture, but since its independence in 2011, data on the actual rain-fed area is lacking. The agricultural sector in the basin contributes one-third of the gross domestic product (GDP) generated across the basin and provides the basis for more than 75 per cent of the employment of the labour force in the basin level.[82] This makes it vital to improve efficiency and productivity in the agriculture sector while also developing other uses for Nile river flows such as hydropower for generating and distributing the electricity needed for development.

The hydropower potential of the Nile basin is estimated at 20 GW, out of which only 26 per cent are currently being tapped.[83] This is even more striking when noting that most riparian countries struggle to meet the national energy demand and the potential social and economic benefits that such hydropower avails. In terms of existing hydropower capacity on the Nile river, Egypt has the highest capacity with 2,100 MW from the High Aswan dam, followed by Ethiopia, the Sudan and Uganda, and Kenya and Rwanda with much lower capacities.[84] Ethiopia has the greatest potential for hydropower and could become the main broker on the Nile river selling power to other countries, thereby offsetting construction costs, meeting domestic energy demand and improving the economic development environment. Uganda, Burundi, the Democratic Republic of Congo, Rwanda, Tanzania and South Sudan are all also looking to avail more power to the domestic and industrial sectors from potential Nile river hydropower.

Hydropower trade has the potential to become a significant industry and driver for development in the Nile basin if appropriate cooperative arrangements are established and supported by a regional transmission grid. Lack of agreements between riparian countries on hydropower projects has hindered the implementation of most power generation and transmission projects. The risk of conflict is amplified by the competing uses of water across the Nile basin both between riparian countries and across different sectors within the same country.

Ethiopia's construction of the Grand Renaissance Dam has generated the greatest potential for conflict in the basin in recent years as the hydropower needs of upstream riparian countries have been considered a serious threat to the water and food security of downstream countries, namely Egypt and the Sudan. The Grand Renaissance Dam has a potential capacity to generate over 5,000 MW, which Ethiopia intends to both use domestically and sell to other riparian countries and neighbouring States. Egypt's main concern was that the water storage reserves required to generate this output would reduce Nile river flows and affect the quantity of water Egypt is able to store in the Aswan High Dam. There was also concern that the non-consumptive use of the Nile river water for the generation of hydropower would actually result in a reduction of Nile river water due to greater evapotranspiration from large water areas now situated closer to the equator and the potential for this stored water to be diverted for irrigation projects upstream. In March 2015, however, Egypt, Ethiopia and the Sudan signed a landmark accord laying out common principles regarding water resource development on the Nile river that takes into account WEF security interests of riparian countries along the basin and helps to mitigate the potential for conflict. Follow-up discussions were held in December 2015.

2. Potential for conflict due to water, energy and food security interests along the Nile river

No management agreement exists covering the entire Nile basin water resources. However, the historic Nile Waters Agreement of 1959 dominated the relationships between riparian countries. It was signed bilaterally by Egypt and the Sudan and regulated the maximum amount of water to be used with 55.5 km^3 allocated for Egypt and 18.5 km^3 allocated for the Sudan.[85] More importantly, the agreement reaffirmed Egypt's veto power on any works on the Nile tributaries or lakes that can cause a harmful drop in water levels to Egypt, a power originally stated in the 1929 Nile Waters Agreement, also concluded between Egypt and the Sudan.[86]

Unfortunately, the 1959 agreement was the source of tension between the signatory parties and the remaining upstream countries. The latter viewed this agreement as unjust as they were not party to it, which denies them equitable access to the Nile river waters for socioeconomic development gains, while Egypt and the Sudan claimed their historical rights to the river's water.

The Nile Basin Initiative (NBI) was subsequently launched in 1999 by the riparian countries with support from the international community. The objective was "to achieve sustainable socio-economic development through equitable utilization of, and benefit from, the common Nile Basin Water resources".[87] The NBI is a transitional body that fosters cooperation between Nile basin countries with the objective of establishing a permanent Nile river basin commission based on the all-inclusive Nile Cooperative Framework Agreement (CFA). The

NBI has succeeded to a certain degree in promoting dialogue, information sharing and cooperative project development but has yet to obtain consensus on a new Nile agreement. Projects facilitated by the NBI have included projects in the WEF sectors from improved water supply networks to better power grid interconnectivity.

Over the last decade, Egypt has also sought to claim that all water of the Nile river, namely the blue water, and all water in the Nile river basin, namely the green water, should be accounted for when determining equitable water shares across riparian countries.[88] By framing the system for analysis at the basin level – as promoted under IWRM principles, Egypt effectively sought to frame the WEF security nexus within a larger system given that the water flowing in the Nile river in the final reaches represents only 5 per cent of total rainfall in the basin.[89] Egypt also framed the issue within the context of water rights, including historical rights, associated with the management of transboundary water resources, rather than focusing on needs alone.

3. Implications of basin-level cooperation on sustainable development with the risk of conflict

The increased stresses on basin resources resulting from a significant population growth and climate change have resulted in lower WEF security. Many riparian countries are looking at the Nile water resources as the catalyst for improved WEF security and the resultant economic development. This increased interest in the Nile river is a potential for conflict in the absence of a basin-wide agreement that not only manages the resources from a water perspective but from a WEF nexus perspective. A human rights-based approach to the nexus allows the deliberations and negotiations on the Nile to put basic human rights first, and particularly the rights of the growing populations of the riparian countries to food, water and development in light of the complexities and uncertainties brought on by climate change. Conflict mitigation in the Nile basin may rest in a holistic management approach that utilizes the WEF security nexus analytical framework in focusing on the shared benefits of a basin-wide management through key entry points such as hydropower trade and regional grid connectivity, improved agricultural performance through improved rain-fed agriculture water management and increased efficiency of existing irrigation systems, and establishing basin-wide institutions for information sharing and dialogue.

D. The Saq-Ram Aquifer System (West)

1. The aquifer and its water

The Saq-Ram Aquifer System (West), also known as the Disi aquifer, is a groundwater basin that extends over a distance of about of 308,000 km^2 from northern Saudi Arabia, where it is known as the Saq aquifer, into Jordan where it is referred to as the Ram Group. The Saq-Ram Aquifer System (West) is identified as the portion from Tabuk-Tayma to the northern border of Jordan.[90] This report deals only with this part of the aquifer as the eastern part (Qassim-Ha'il) is not considered to have any direct transboundary relevance.

Map 5. The Saq-Ram Aquifer System exploitable area with irrigation areas and energy use for groundwater pumping

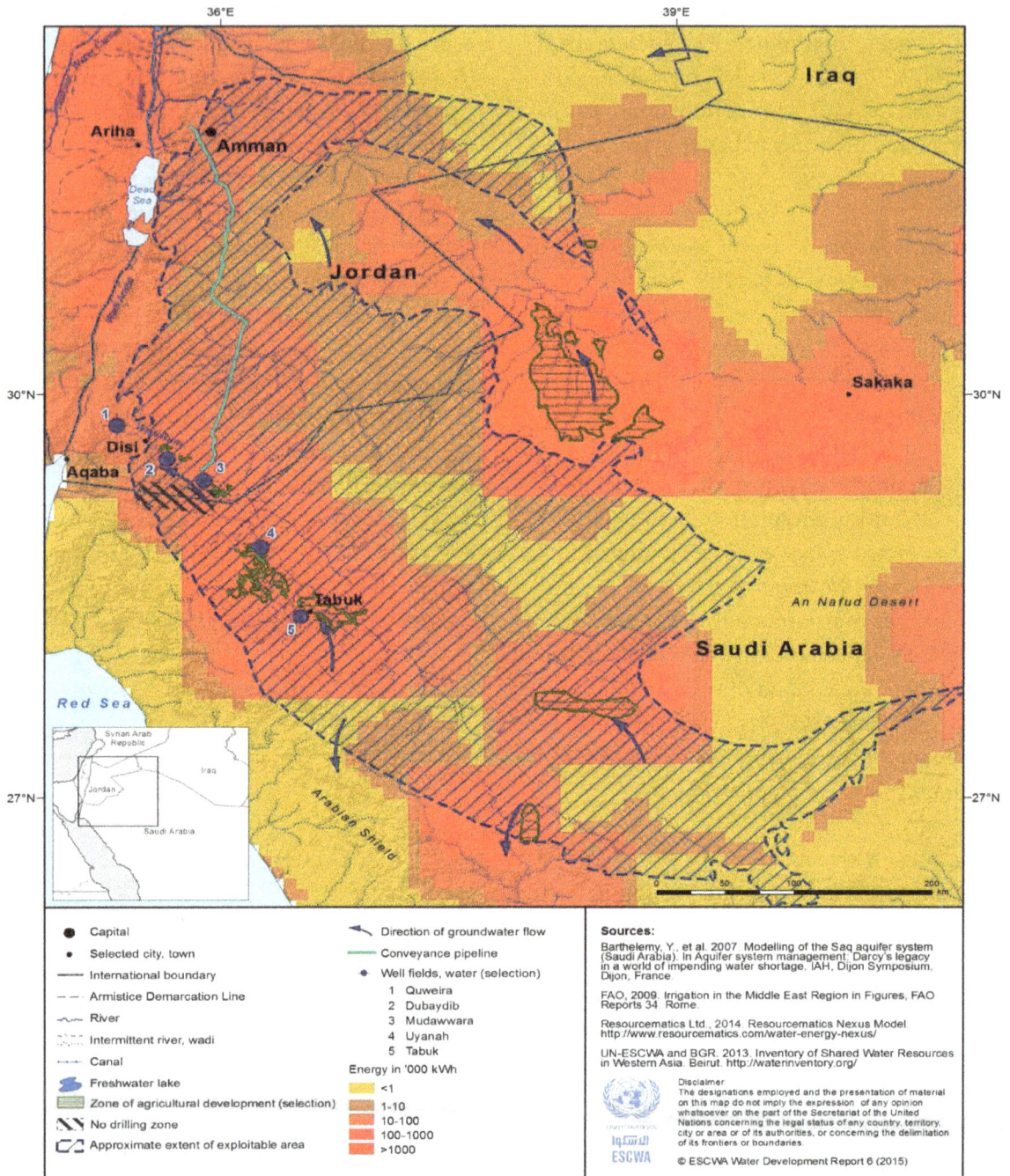

Sources: Barthelemy, and others, 2007; FAO, 2009c; Resourcematics Ltd., 2014; ESCWA and BGR, 2013.

In its western part, which stretches along the eastern margins of the Arabian shield (map 5), the aquifer system is unconfined with outcrops extending from central Saudi Arabia to the Dead Sea in western Jordan. In the eastern part, it is confined. The paleorecharge rate of the system was 3.5 mm/year during the pluvial period. Current climatic conditions of the region limit the recharge rate to 3-10 MCM/year.[91] The Ministry of Agriculture and Water (MOAW) in Saudi Arabia estimates the groundwater reserve of the Saq aquifer at 65 billion m^3, 4-10 BCM of which are located under Jordanian territory.[92] In terms of flow regime, the water in the Saq-Ram Aquifer System (West) used to move from the Tabuk-Tayma area in Saudi Arabia passing Al Jafr to its natural discharge zone, the Dead Sea (map 5). However, after 1980, the increased abstraction of groundwater in the Tabuk region altered the general flow pattern in the system.[93]

The quality of the basin water is generally considered good and does not limit exploitability. However, the groundwater shows a natural presence of radionuclides, which can be eliminated through a costly treatment process. Based on estimates, people who drink two litres of water a day from the Saq-Ram Aquifer System may be exposed to unsafe radiation levels much higher than the World Health Organization (WHO) standard.[94] Saudi Arabia currently treats fossil groundwater from the basin to remove radioactive particles. In Jordan, the Ministry of Water and Irrigation (MWI) stated that its tests produced much lower results and that the water is being blended with clean water from other sources to bring down radioactivity levels to WHO standards.[95]

2. Food and water nexus

The absence of significant quantities of surface water or renewable groundwater in Jordan and Saudi Arabia makes both countries dependent on non-renewable groundwater. Jordan began abstraction from the Ram Group in 1977 at a rate of 5.4 MCM/year for various uses. By 2001, 55 MCM/year were being abstracted for agricultural purposes and 15 MCM/year for municipal supply, bringing the total abstraction rate to 70 MCM/year. In 2008, it was reduced to 60 MCM/year of which 40 MCM were used for irrigation and 20 MCM for domestic use.[96] Since 2013, 100 MCM/year are being extracted to supply the Disi-Amman Water Conveyance Project.

Saudi Arabia's total abstraction rate in 1980 from the Saq aquifer was approximately 890 MCM by 2005, it had risen to 5,708 MCM/year. However, more than 80 per cent of these abstractions take place in the eastern Qassim-Ha'il region, which is not considered relevant in the transboundary context with Jordan. In 2008, the abstraction from the Saq aquifer in the north-western Tabuk region amounted to 1,053 MCM; equivalent to 20 per cent of Saudi Arabia's total abstraction from the Saq aquifer.[97]

In Tabuk, most of the irrigated area grows annual crops, including wheat, potatoes, onions, and alfalfa. Most of the farming in the region is undertaken by the Tabuk Agricultural Development Company (TADCO). The company has 260 wells that penetrate the Saq aquifer, many of which are directly connected to circular sprinkler pivot irrigation systems,[98] which work at approximately 60 per cent efficiency due to high wind drift and evaporation losses.[99] The agricultural census for the Tabuk region shows that a total of 137,800 ha are utilized for growing crops, which has remained fairly constant since 1995. However, water abstraction continued to increase, which was most likely due to the increasing cultivation of summer crops and water-intensive crops such as fodder. Wheat cultivation in the Tabuk region decreased significantly between 1989-1998, mainly due to the Government's reduction of fixed wheat prices in 1994. Coincidentally, annual fodder cultivation in the Tabuk region increased tenfold during the same period.[100] Thus, although wheat production was reduced, abstraction from the Saq aquifer continued to increase. By 2006, wheat production had gradually risen again to equate to 55 per cent of the total area of crops in Tabuk.[101]

In 2008, 990 MCM water was used for irrigating the Tabuk region, equating to 94 per cent of the total amount abstracted from the Saq.[102] Based on new policies introduced in 2008 that aimed to conserve water, Saudi Arabia is reducing its total wheat production by 12.5 per cent annually and all local wheat production will stop by 2016.[103] The Ministry of Water and Electricity (MOWE) of Saudi Arabia also suggested an overall reduction of 50 per cent in agricultural water demand in the Tabuk area.[104]

In the Disi-Mudawwara region of south-western Jordan, five large-scale farming companies were licensed to abstract water from the Ram Group in order to irrigate a total of 11,676 ha.[105] Research by the Jordan University of Science and Technology shows that large-scale agriculture in the Disi-Mudawwara region requires much more intensive irrigation than anywhere else in Jordan. On average, under irrigated conditions, one kilogram of wheat produced in the Disi region requires 3.5 times more water than in other regions in Jordan.[106] According to the MWI in Jordan, irrigation efficiency is poor, water tariffs can hardly recover the operation cost of the delivered water and the pricing of groundwater is ineffective at promoting conservative use.[107] Most of the products cultivated, such as potatoes, are considered low-cash crops, yet, over 65 per cent of the country's water budget is used for irrigation. Jordan also sells virtual water to its neighbouring countries in the form of vegetable exports without holistically considering the economic value of the embedded water being exported and the importance of water security in such a water-poor country as Jordan.

In order to reallocate fresh water for domestic purposes, 17 per cent of Jordan's annual irrigation water is treated wastewater.[108] Furthermore, in order to stabilize abstraction, the Jordanian Government had plans to reduce agricultural abstractions from the Ram Group in Disi after 2011 when its contracts with the main agricultural companies in the area expired.[109] However, until 2013, agricultural companies were still abstracting from the aquifer in the Disi region.[110]

3. Water and energy nexus

In 2013, Jordan completed the construction of the Disi-Amman Water Conveyance Project, a pipeline system designed to extract water from the Ram Group through 55 production wells in the Dubaydib well field (map 5), The system is intended to supply Amman with an average of 100 MCM/year of water for a period of at least 25 years. The water is pumped as far as 325 km and is lifted a total of 800 m requiring about 4kW/m³ of energy for horizontal and vertical pumping. The system requires a total of 50 MW per year or nearly 2 per cent of Jordan's total annual electricity demand and satisfies about 40 per cent of Jordan's annual water needs.[111] According to Jordan's National Electric Power Company (NEPCO), the water sector is the single largest consumer of electricity in the country; pumping, transport, distribution, and wastewater management amount to approximately 15 per cent of the total national electricity demand.[112]

According to the MWI in Jordan, climate change will lead to a 30 per cent decrease in the country's water availability in the next 20 years.[113] Furthermore, within the next 10 years, industrial water demand is expected to increase by 300 per cent and commercial demand by 200 per cent.[114] The country's energy strategy in 2007 aimed to have 30 per cent of its national demand covered from nuclear power by 2030 and 14 per cent from national oil shale reserves by 2020,[115] both increasing the demand on water resources. The Majdal area in the northern Al Mafraq Governorate has been chosen as location for the first nuclear reactor, where treated wastewater from the municipal Khirbet Samra Treatment Plant is planned to be used for cooling the reactors.[116] Jordan planned to begin mining for uranium, reserves of which are estimated to be 65,000 tons, in the country's central region by 2015.[117] The Jordan Atomic Energy Commission stated that uranium mining would require approximately 60 MCM/year of water.[118]

Other energy prospects are related to oil shale deposits. Current estimates show that Jordan holds the equivalent of 40-70 billion barrels of

oil in shale deposits.[119] Over 23 shale oil fields have been examined, most of which are located in central Jordan. Eesti Energia, the company contracted to mine the shale oil from the El Lajjun and Attarat deposits, states that 1.8 barrels of water are required to process one barrel of oil shale using the Enefit processing technology. Oil shale processing will rely on water from a local aquifer in the Attarat region.[120] Additionally, Jordan has granted rights to Royal Dutch Shell to test its in situ processing technology in the Azraq and Al Jafr regions, which is considered to require substantive volumes of water with the Saq-Ram Aquifer System being one possible source. The water demand for shale oil mining in Jordan is unlikely to have any significant direct impact on water availability in Saudi Arabia.

4. Transboundary impacts of abstraction

Both Jordan and Saudi Arabia have proportionally abstracted significant quantities of groundwater from the Saq-Ram Aquifer System (West) and have depleted the resource to an alarming point with an ever-increasing energy demand to pump the water from deeper levels, as seen in map 5, particularly affecting agricultural areas that rely on groundwater pumping. The groundwater levels in Jordan have dropped at an average rate of 2.3-10.5 m/year.[121] The simulated drawdown for the recently added Dubaydib well field is about 2 m/year with a dynamic drawdown that may reach 100 m in 25 years. This would bring the groundwater levels down to about 350 metres below ground level, making any further extraction economically unviable.[122] In the Tabuk area, if abstraction continues at its current rate, 71 per cent of the Saq's exploitable reserve will be consumed by 2055.[123]

In the case of a transboundary aquifer, such as the Saq-Ram aquifer, the closer the well fields are to the national border, the more likely they are to restrict their neighbours' ability to abstract groundwater themselves. For example, in the Tabuk area, the large volumes abstracted for irrigation have created huge cones of depression that locally divert the generally north-easterly groundwater flow direction. As a result, the 140 MCM/year of groundwater that once flowed across the border to Jordan have been reduced to negligible amounts.[124] Groundwater levels will continue to decline in south-western Jordan as abstraction from the Tabuk area persists. In theory, the abstractions in Jordan would have the same impact on Saudi Arabia but since abstractions are significantly less in the Disi-Mudawwara region than in Tabuk, the transboundary consequences are likely to be less significant.[125]

5. Transboundary cooperation in past and present

In the 1980s and 1990s, the Saq Aquifer in Saudi Arabia and the Ram Group in Jordan were studied separately. It was only in recent years that studies began to focus on the assessment of the Saq-Ram Aquifer System (West) as a potential transboundary aquifer.[126] To date, no official treaty has been signed between the aquifer States to regulate abstraction behaviour. In 2007, however, the MWI in Jordan and the MOWE in Saudi Arabia signed a non-binding Memorandum of Understanding (MoU) that established a 10 km no-drill zone along both sides of the national border between the Dubaydib and Tabuk well fields (map 5).[127] The agreement prohibits the drilling of new production wells and the expansion of current

agricultural activities in the defined zone but, since it is non-binding, it does not constitute a treaty under international law. Starting with the 2007 agreement, both aquifer States have had the opportunity to enhance water cooperation through improved monitoring and the exchange of data. Previous studies on both sides could provide a useful basis for future joint research and monitoring efforts.[128]

A consultation mechanism with experts from both States could be established to facilitate joint research efforts that would allow the individual countries to make informed decisions in the future. An analytical nexus framework is necessary to capture all interactions.

E. North-West Sahara Aquifer System

1. The aquifer and its water

The North-Western Sahara Aquifer System (NWSAS) is a multilayered groundwater reservoir that extends over an area of 1 million km^2. Geographically, 60 per cent is located in Algeria, 30 per cent in Libya and the remaining 10 per cent in Tunisia.[129] The system is composed of two primary reservoirs that are superposed and partially connected, each with distinct hydrogeological features. The Complex Terminal (CT) represents the upper part of the system, a confined aquifer that extends over 600,000 km^2.[130] The Continental Intercalaire (CI) is the lower mostly confined aquifer extending over an area of 1 million km^2.[131]

The replenishment of the entire NWSAS is estimated at only 1 km^3/year (on average 1 mm/year), meaning that the aquifer can be considered non-renewable. The thickness of its aquifer units has favoured the accumulation of large quantities of non-renewable water during the last pluvial period in the Pleistocene and early Holocene. Water quality and limited accessibility reduce the water exploitability of the aquifer to only 1,280 km³.[132] The water in the system is fairly stagnant, moving at less than 1 m/year with a pattern of flow from the inner continental regions of Algeria and Libya towards the eastern coast of Tunisia.[133] In fact, the NWSAS transboundary aquifer system is located in an area without any significant surface water; therefore, any water use in the region depends primarily on groundwater.

Until the 1970s, water abstractions were insignificant, less than the recharge and within the aquifer sustainable yield. During the 1980s, the technological progress in well drilling increased the accessibility to groundwater at depth. A 2001 census identified 8,800 wells extracting water from the NWSAS, mostly for irrigation purposes. 6,500 of these wells are located in Algeria and have a combined abstraction rate of 1.3 km³/year, 1,200 wells are in Tunisia with an abstraction rate of 0.55 km³/year and 1,100 in Libya with an estimated abstraction of 0.33 km³/year.[134] Currently, the total rate of extraction from NWSAS is approximately 2.2 to 2.5 km³/year and is rapidly increasing.[135]

2. Agriculture and food production

Up to 90 per cent of all abstracted water is used for irrigation purposes in Libya, followed by 86 per cent in Tunisia and 60 per cent in Algeria.[136] In the chotts region of Tunisia,[137] artesian aquifers have made the cultivation of dates for

export economically viable. Currently, 90 per cent of Tunisia's national dates are produced in the chotts region, which requires approximately 1.5 km³/year of water.[138] After 1995, artesian aquifers that once provided the region with free water disappeared. Since then, water is pumped from the aquifer by the regional water authority and is distributed to farmers once a week at 20 to 25 per cent of the real cost.[139]

Three years after establishing the 2000 national agricultural development programme, Algeria began to shift from being a net food importer to becoming an exporter, with date palms the single largest agricultural export product. Most of the national date production takes place in nine Saharan wilayas, of which the five most productive ones depend on the NWSAS for water.[140] Unlike Algeria and Tunisia, which invested in the agricultural sector for the purpose of exports, Libya used water in an attempt to achieve national food security. Libya began major agricultural projects in the 1990s for which groundwater was abstracted from an aquifer in the south-east and transferred to the northern coastal areas in order to grow cereals, fruits and vegetables. An important question for Libya is if energy-intensive abstraction and the transfer of non-renewable groundwater for agriculture is the most economical option, especially when oil and gas revenues could provide the basis for imports that could contribute to national food security.[141]

3. Water for energy versus energy for water

For conventional oil or gas abstractions, large volumes of water are injected to keep up reservoir pressure and are used in downstream petroleum production processes. Algeria, Libya

50

and Tunisia are all extracting fossil fuels in the NWSAS area. Libya and Tunisia produce oil in the Ghadames basin and are planning to expand operations.[142, 143] Several companies have plans for prospecting, operating or expanding the production of oil and natural gas in the Ghadames basin, implying a more intense exploitation of water resources from NWSAS by all three riparian States.[144]

In 2013, the United States Department of Energy estimated the availability of shale gas reserves in south-east Algeria at 19.8 BCM.[145] Different estimates relate such volumes of gas to a respective total water demand of between 5.4[146] and 6.0[147] BCM. The potential impacts of shale gas development are currently under public discussion in Algeria, including the question whether the available groundwater is sufficient to embark on a water-intensive hydraulic fracturing operation without impacting other such water-demanding sectors as agriculture. The location of major shale gas fields in the NWSAS area suggests that Algeria may need to double its water abstraction rate in order to support its shale gas development plans. Already in 2011, Sonatrach, the Algerian national hydrocarbons company, had drilled exploratory boreholes for shale gas.[148]

Since NWSAS is considered a non-renewable aquifer, a full depletion of the aquifer reserves is inevitable in the long term if extractions continue to increase. Consequently, social, economic and environmental impacts will be felt long before the resource is at risk of exhaustion. The exploitation NWSAS has experienced over the past 30 years has had a serious impact on some of the system's hydrogeological features. Since parts of the NWSAS lie below salt lakes, groundwater resources are vulnerable to salt water contamination through downward percolation, which would eventually impact on the energy required for the remediation of more saline groundwater. Another consequence of large abstractions is the loss of pressure in artesian aquifers, which will reflect on the amount of energy required for lifting or pumping the groundwater. For example, north of the chotts in the Biskra region, 45×10^6 m³/year of water is provided by 13 deep artesian wells at no expense; however, if the artesian pressure was to be reduced, an estimated 13 million euros per year would be required for pumping the water from these wells.[149]

4. Future water use perspectives

An awareness of the factors impacting NWSAS have led all three States to reform their respective national water policies, focusing on tackling inefficiencies in water management by transitioning to Integrated Water Resources Management (IWRM) policies. This led to the adoption of the Letter of Sector Development Policy, a tool to better manage and monitor the aquifers.[150] Tunisia is already aiming to stabilize its current water abstraction rate, whereas Algeria and Libya are still planning to increase their abstractions. Algeria has plans based on two scenarios: a "weak scenario" under which it would increase its extraction from 0.55 km³/year to 1.36 km³/year, and a "strong scenario" that suggests an increase to 1.86 km³/year. Libya also plans to extract an additional 90 km³/year to supply its Great Manmade River Project;[151] however, the current conflict may no longer allow for such plans.

5. Transboundary impacts

Because of the ample water reserves in the NWSAS, it may currently not be considered urgent to address the potential impacts of overextraction. However, as quantities shrink over time, any increasing water demand will lead to more competitive situations. The need to cooperate may differ between the neighbouring aquifer States depending on how each State is impacted by the actual or planned exploitation. For example, plans in Libya to increase exploitation have been estimated to cause a drawdown of 50 m in both Algeria and Tunisia; the "strong scenario" expansion plans in Algeria may lead to 200-300 m drawdown on the Tunisian side.[152] Hence, Tunisia may be seen as having the strongest incentive to seek cooperation with its neighbours since it is more directly impacted by both Algerian and Libyan abstractions. Moreover, Libya seems to have less incentive to cooperate with its neighbours since its exploitations are unlikely to be impacted by abstraction plans of neither Algeria nor Tunisia.[153]

6. Cooperation in past, present and future and potential links to the water-energy-food nexus

In the mid-1970s, the riparian countries of the NWSAS began two- and, later, three-way discussions concerning the management of shared groundwater resources. This led to the mutual agreement of a systematic programme for the exchange of hydrogeological information and joint monitoring of the aquifers.[154] In 1998, the Observatory for Sahara and the Sahel (OSS), an organization that seeks to combat desertification, obtained support from the Swiss Agency for Development and Cooperation (SDC),

the International Fund for Agricultural Development (IFAD) and the United Nations Food and Agricultural Organization (FAO) to implement a three-year cooperative study on the NWSAS.[155] The study focused on the parameters of the aquifers, setting up a shared geographic information system (GIS) database, and later developing a mathematical model of the basin to serve as a management tool for the water authorities to simulate how each aquifer would respond to future development schemes.[156]

After the end of the three-year project in 2002, the concerned countries agreed to mutually finance a consultation mechanism facilitated by the OSS in the form of a steering committee comprised of representatives from the respective water authorities of each country. The main goals of the steering committee are to manage and update the GIS database and the simulation model; to develop and publish indicators on the use of water resources; and promote and facilitate the implementation of joint studies and research.[157] While, in principle, this consultation mechanism can be considered a starting point and an expandable framework for trilateral cooperation on the shared groundwater, it is important to clarify that the committee is strictly a communication tool for joint research efforts aiming to allow the individual countries to make informed decisions in the future. It is not a trilateral agreement on joint management and, therefore, negates any provisions that legally obligate any of the countries to limit their abstractions in consideration of the impact they may have on their neighbour's ability to access the resource.[158]

The existing cooperation mechanisms for joint research under the OSS offer a good potential in the future for further multisectoral research projects and studies within the perspective of a WEF security nexus analytical framework. Currently, ECE, in cooperation with the Global Water Partnership Mediterranean (GWP-Med) and OSS, is planning for a nexus study based on the draft transboundary river basin nexus assessment methodology.[159] Eventually, the OSS-coordinated mechanism could further develop into an intergovernmental basin commission that may assist in governing and managing the fair use and conservation of the resource between the three aquifer States to achieve long-term sustainability.[160] If so, examining the various efforts in resource use would benefit from considering a human rights-based approach to WEF security.

III. Energy and Water Interdependencies for Improved Services

This chapter further explores the interdependencies of energy and water in the light of energy endowment differences in the region, affecting sustainable development goals in general and services delivery in particular, and proposes the nexus approach to foster greater efficiency and technological innovation in the energy sector. The dependency on desalination is examined through the available technologies and efficiencies. Alternative energy sources including nuclear energy are considered within a nexus framework in order to evaluate each source and its interlinkages with other natural resources.

A. Overview

1. Overview of energy endowments in the Arab region

In 2013, the total share of global crude oil production in Arab countries was estimated to be 30.5 per cent and that of natural gas 16 per cent. For the same year, the region's share of the world's proven oil and gas reserves were estimated to be 55.8 per cent and 27.3 per cent, respectively.[161] However, conventional energy resources are unequally distributed among Arab countries and are largely used unsustainably.

Total primary energy consumption in Arab countries has steadily increased at an average annual growth rate of 5.0 per cent over the period 2003-2013, with a slightly higher rate, namely, 6.3 per cent, for the GCC countries.[162] The part of the total primary energy production devoted to satisfy the region's energy demand has increased from approximately 31 per cent in 2003 to approximately 40 per cent in 2013; for the GCC countries, this ratio increased from approximately 25 per cent to approximately 33 per cent over the same period. The region is steadily shifting from its historical role of energy supplier to increasingly demanding energy. These trends are further intensified by the low conventional energy prices that are mainly driven by substantial direct and indirect subsidies. A large proportion of energy consumption is due to energy inefficiencies at the production, distribution and end-use levels. In 2012, Arab countries used approximately twice the amount of energy that the world used to produce the same amount of GDP and approximately three times that of the member countries of the Organisation for Economic Co-operation and Development (OECD).[163]

Energy efficiency can result in using less energy to provide the same service, or using the same amount of energy to provide more services. As indicated, there is a large untapped potential of energy efficiency gains across all economic sectors, which is available in the region and can, according to some estimates, allow to reduce the primary energy consumption by more than 25 per cent by 2030, even in a conservative low-policy intensity scenario, which corresponds to about 50 per cent of total current consumption in the region. If a more aggressive technical potential scenario is pursued, the region could potentially reduce projected primary energy consumption by more than 50 per cent in 2030.[164] The potential energy savings can be considered as an alternative source of energy supply for the region at a very competitive cost; in addition, there will be many associated benefits in terms of the water saved in the production of this energy, not to mention environmental, economic and social impacts.[165]

Morever, the region has significant potential for renewable energy, mainly solar but also wind and to a lesser extent hydro and geothermal energy that can be tapped as sustainable energy resources.

An Arab strategic framework was developed to provide a roadmap for the development of renewable energy in the region,[166] which was adopted by the League of Arab States in January 2013. It is estimated that if all Arab countries accomplish the targets agreed upon, including concerning hydropower, the contribution of renewable energy will increase to reach 75 GW of installed power generation capacities by 2030. This figure represents approximately 30 per cent of the total installed electrical capacity of 2013.[167, 168] Substantial targets have also been announced for solar domestic water heating, which is another

untapped source of renewable energy, either in terms of installed capacity or collector areas.[169]

Other largely untapped applications of renewable energy sources in the region are decentralized direct uses of renewable energy, such as water pumping, space and process heating, food drying, and small-scale off-grid photovoltaic (PV) systems dedicated to specific services, such as lighting and telecommunication, among others. These direct uses of renewable energy sources, if widely implemented through appropriate dissemination programmes, can be a valuable means for providing energy services to rural and remote areas at a reasonable economic cost.

2. Access to energy services

Large disparities exist among Arab countries regarding levels of total primary energy consumption per capita and electrical consumption per capita. Total primary energy consumption in 2012 (kg of oil equivalent (KOE) per capita per year) varied between 3,390 and 15,824 for the seven countries with the highest levels of total energy consumption per capita, 148 to 262 for the three countries with the lowest levels of total energy consumption per capita, and 308 to 1,290 for the remaining countries. Similar inequalities can be noted in terms of electrical consumption per capita.[170] To a certain extent, these disparities reflect the lack of access to adequate energy services in many countries in the region, not to mention their specific effect on related water and irrigation services that depend on this energy and on achieving sustainable development in general.

Box 3. Regional electricity networks for improved energy security

The Arab region is subconnected through three regional electricity grids that allow trade of surplus electricity between countries and more recently act as a pathway for renewable wind and solar resources in an attempt to improve supply security through diversification of sources. The three grids, which are not yet interconnected, include: the Comelec or Maghreb interconnection from Morocco to Tunisia (including Algeria, Libya, Mauritania, Morocco, and Tunisia); the EIJLLPST network from Libya to Turkey, including Egypt, Iraq, Jordan, Lebanon, Libya, the State of Palestine, Syrian Arab Republic and Turkey, with the Sudan requesting to join this network through a connection with Egypt); and the GCC Interconnection Authority (GCCIA) for the GCC countries. Projects are also underway with plans for several interconnections between these grids and Europe through underwater cables. Although these grids have existed for some time (since the 1950s in the case of the Maghreb grid), electricity trade among Arab countries has remained below expectations for several reasons, which include limited generation reserves, the absence of harmonized regulatory frameworks, and institutional weaknesses. However, renewed motivation for regional trade is expected as part of resources motivation in connection with renewable energy sources, namely, mostly wind and solar energy.

Sources: Arab Ministerial Council of Electricity, 2015; Hafner, Tagliapietra and el Andaloussi, 2012.

Although mainly in rural areas, 65 per cent of the population in the Sudan and 48 per cent in Yemen are not supplied with electricity.[171] Moreover, energy supply and services in the State of Palestine are frequently disrupted by the Israeli embargo and unstable security situation, rendering energy security and access to energy services from available local renewable resources one of the main issues to be looked at. The lack of access to reliable and sustainable energy services in other countries aggravates the cycle of extreme poverty for vulnerable social groups, especially in rural areas and some peri-urban locations, and impairs the ability to improve social and economic conditions. This, in turn, adversely impacts access to basic goods and services.

However, the six GCC countries have been cooperating for over a decade to improve the efficiency and stability of their power supply through an interconnection that links their national electric power networks and supports trade in energy services.

3. Nexus thinking as an approach for fostering greater support for energy efficiency and renewable energy options

Water and energy are closely linked: water is needed to extract conventional energy resources and generate electricity; and energy is needed to extract, distribute, collect, and treat used water. The sustainable supply of energy and water is essential in supporting sustainable economic development. Without adequate access to both of them, no economic or social development can take place. However, due to the demographic expansion and a long history of unsustainable use of energy and water, affordable supplies of water and energy are becoming increasingly difficult to get, and environmental issues, including pollution and climate change, have been intrinsically linked with the unsustainable use of water and energy.

Only sustainable solutions can address these issues in the most effective manner. They require that water and energy issues are tackled using a systemic integrated approach for managing water and energy resources, which should take into consideration the key roles and responsibilities associated with the management, operation and use of these resources. This includes public institutions, industry and end users.

A sustainable systemic approach should lead to optimizing the use of water and energy by doing the following:

- Reducing the conventional energy requirements needed for extracting, producing and transporting irrigation and potable water, and transporting and treating wastewater. This should primarily be achieved by promoting energy efficiency in all of these processes, including enforcing minimum equipment energy efficiency requirements and smart grid water distribution and pumping systems through the use of appropriate technologies. It also involves using renewable energy sources wherever it is feasible and resorting to waste-to-energy schemes in wastewater treatment plants;
- Reducing unaccounted-for water losses, namely water lost during transportation and distribution through networks, and optimizing the different water requirements by promoting sustainable irrigation systems and the availability of environmentally sound water in all processes and for individual utilization.

Furthermore, managing the water and energy resources in a more sustainable manner is inherently interrelated and any positive impact on either of the two resources will impact positively on the other. A systemic approach should consider the WEF nexus to promote rational decision-making regarding the national and eventually regional choices with respect to these three strategic pillars. The decision-making process should recognize the interwoven concerns of WEF policies and examine the three sectors as part of an interrelated system.

4. Sustainable Energy for All

In 2012, the United Nations General Assembly declared 2014-2024 as the United Nations Decade of Sustainable Energy for All (SE4All).[172] The initiative aims to catalyse actions around three clear objectives to be achieved by 2030:

- Ensuring universal access to modern energy services;
- Doubling the global rate of improvement in energy efficiency with respect to 2010;
- Doubling the share of renewable energy in the global energy mix with respect to 2010.

These three important objectives are intrinsically interrelated and reinforce each other in many instances. Energy-efficient systems and equipment require much less energy to provide the same services, allowing the saved energy to be directed to other users and end uses. In addition, the reduced energy requirements at the end-use level help renewable energy solutions to reach a higher share in the energy mix. Moreover, renewable energy solutions, whether in their direct applications, namely, solar water heating, PV and wind pumping, and so on, or in their use to generate electricity in decentralized or centralized systems, provide additional means to supply more end users with energy services.

Achieving the three objectives together will maximize economic and social development benefits and help stabilize climate change in the long run. In fact, a nexus approach to the water and energy issues can substantially contribute to the achievement of all three SE4All objectives.

B. Water use in energy and electricity production

1. Alternative energy sources and supply in the Arab region

Alternative energy sources and supplies that are available and accessible in the Arab region include solar and wind renewable energy sources, biomass and biofuels, unconventional hydrocarbon sources, and energy savings that can be generated from improvements in energy efficiency.

(a) Renewable energy resources

Renewable energy sources indigenous to the region include solar thermal energy sources for process heat and power generation; solar PV systems in a decentralized or centralized configuration; wind energy for direct mechanical use or decentralized/centralized power production; hydropower generated through massive dams or modular units on rivers and streams; and geothermal energy, which is only available in some of the countries in the region.

Most countries in the Arab region have significant solar and wind energy potential. The recent global reductions in the cost of

renewable energy technologies, such as PV panels and wind turbines, have made some of these technologies competitive and economical, even for net energy exporting countries when national energy accounts are considered. However, upscaling the development of renewable energy sources for centralized power generation requires the development of smart grids at the national level. Smart grids are required to stabilize intermittent input from renewable energy systems associated with the substantial relative variation of the energy input into the grid. This will also require the development of strong interconnecting networks between the countries in the region and effective power exchange agreements in order to allow the surplus of energy production to be transferred where it is needed across national boundaries. However, it should be noted that, from a WEF nexus perspective, the renewable energy technologies used in power generation from solar thermal sources require similar amounts of water for cooling and steam generation as conventional thermal power generation technologies.

Other renewable energy applications include upscaling the development of decentralized grids connected to small- to medium-scale renewable energy power generating systems, such as through a net metering scheme, promoting the development of decentralized systems for direct uses of renewable energy, and the development of small-scale off-grid renewable energy systems for power supply to one or more end users, or to specific energy services. These applications can, in some countries in the region, offer valuable alternatives for providing energy services to a variety of end users, especially in remote rural locations.

58

(b) Biomass and biofuels

Biomass resources in the region include wood, residual material from agricultural and forestry processes and organic industrial, human and animal wastes. Different technologies can be used to transform biomass resources into clean forms of energy, including biofuels. For instance, waste-to-energy technologies can generate secondary sources of energy, while providing a significant reduction in the quantities of waste that require final disposal, therefore positively contributing to the more effective waste management schemes.[173] Many Arab countries, including Egypt, Morocco and Tunisia, have already started using second generation biofuels in the energy mix of some industrial facilities; many others, such as Jordan, Saudi Arabia, Tunisia, and the United Arab Emirates, are using methane generated from landfills to produce electricity.[174]

Furthermore, gaseous or liquid biofuels can be produced from selected crops, wild plants or algae, crop residues, agro-industrial wastes and urban wastes. Liquid biofuels are used mainly in the transport sector, with bioethanol and biodiesels amongst the most widely used biofuels worldwide, with sugar canes and corn widely used as a feedstock to produce bioethanol in Brazil and the United States. However, these two sources of feedstock are not sustainable in the Arab region, since their production would diminish important arable land and fresh water resources from other high-priority uses needed to support food security objectives. Accordingly, oil-bearing crops, such as jatropha, which can be grown on marginal and degraded land, are being considered as a potential alternative source of biofuel in the region.[175]

Another promising new track that involves desert algae for biofuel is being investigated in some of the Gulf countries, including Saudi Arabia and the United Arab Emirates.[176] Various complex environmental impacts can be associated with bioenergy production. These impacts can be positive in terms of waste management or negative in terms of impact or arable land and fresh water resources depending on the type of biomass used as feedstock, local conditions, efficiency and intensity of the biomass use, and associated inputs used in the bioenergy production.

(c) Unconventional hydrocarbon energy sources

Unconventional oils and gases include all hydrocarbon resources that are difficult to extract because of their location on the ground or their nature that makes them difficult to produce. The liquids category includes heavy and extraheavy oils, shale oils, and tar shales and tar sands. The natural gases category includes shale gas, tight gas from compact reservoirs, coalbed methane gas, and, in the long term, methane hydrates.

Arab countries account for more than 7,000 trillion cubic feet (TCF) of unconventional hydrocarbon resources, with such countries as Jordan and Morocco actively preparing for the exploitation of oil shale.[177] Others, such as Oman, Saudi Arabia and perhaps Algeria, may be the first countries to exploit unconventional shale gas.[178]

Hydrofracking is used for both shale oil and shale gas and raises public concerns about groundwater pollution and extended land use. In situ technologies for processing oil shale can be harmful to groundwater while other oil shale processing technologies require large amounts of water.[179] Indeed, hydrofracking is a water-intensive activity, where a mixture composed of 80 per cent water, sand and chemicals is used to facilitate fracturing and increase the permeability of the shale.[180] Furthermore, it takes 2.6 to 4 barrels of water to produce one barrel of oil from oil shale, and 2.3 to 5.8 barrels of water for one barrel of oil from oil sands. A shale gas well can use 2 to 4 million gallons of water to drill and fracture, with one report indicating that shale gas production requires up to four times the amount of water usually consumed by conventional natural gas.[181]

(d) Energy efficiency improvements for energy savings

Finally, the large, virtual energy supply that could result from a considerable reduction in the significant energy inefficiencies could create large amounts of energy for other end users or provide additional services at very competitive costs. Energy efficiency is the most cost-effective source of energy, based on national accounts balances, with an associated net positive impact on the social and economic levels, the environment and existing water resources. Policies and standards need to be developed, or reinforced, in order to promote efficiency improvements, particularly in processes and applications related to the water-energy nexus, including:[182]

- Desalination processes;
- Water and wastewater pumping, including equipment energy efficiency requirements, and smart grid water distribution and pumping systems involving variable speed motors and appropriate monitoring and control systems;
- Aeration in biological treatment systems and operation of anaerobic digesters;
- Water loss in the water distribution systems;
- Demand-side management, including smart irrigation systems, water heating systems, other building or household equipment using or dispensing water, and consumer behaviour.

2. Solar, nuclear and wind energy

Alternative energy sources must be analysed within the WEF security nexus analytical framework from the perspective of integrated natural resources management. In view of climate change, solar, wind and nuclear energy sources are being considered in the Arab region as the main sources of alternative energy in the hope of diversifying the electricity generation mix away from hydrocarbons. Such energy sources have their own set of challenges and potential synergies when considered within the WEF security nexus.

The water demand tied within alternative energy sources can vary from the limited cleaning requirement of PV panels, the higher demand of concentrated solar plants and up to the cooling demands of nuclear power plants. Cooling demands can further vary according to new technologies such as dry cooling and hybrid systems. Similarly, land requirements can vary from small to large for nuclear power plants and solar energy respectively.

The prerequisites for a nuclear power plant are complex and range from geopolitical, institutional and legal frameworks to the selection of technology. There are currently no operational nuclear power plants in the Arab region, but several nuclear projects are in progress. Countries that are publicly seeking or currently implementing nuclear power plants programmes at various stages include Algeria, Egypt, Jordan, Saudia Arabia, the Sudan,[183] and the United Arab Emirates.[184] Other countries such as the Syrian Arab Republic and Yemen have also shown interest, but due to current security concerns plans have dwindled without any development. Kuwait had the intent to build nuclear power reactors by 2022, but the Kuwaiti Government, largely influenced by the Fukushima incident, reversed its policy on nuclear energy and abandoned nuclear energy for power generation. Oman and Qatar have only signed nuclear cooperation agreements with Russia. For Bahrain, nuclear power does not present an option in view of its electric grid. Morocco and Tunisia are currently undertaking a feasibility study in the field of nuclear energy for desalination. Statements regarding plans to establish nuclear power plants for Iraq and Lebanon are currently unavailable.

Generally, solar technologies have a promising potential in the Arab region due to its high solar irradiance. Solar technologies can be divided into two main types, solar photovoltaic energy and solar thermal energy. Solar photovoltaic energy can be further divided into several types, including solar photovoltaic (PV), concentrated photovoltaic (CPV) and high concentrated photovoltaic (HCPV). As concerns PV, the water demand is low and mainly associated with cleaning while demand is higher for CPV and HCPV systems, which are associated with cooling. Solar thermal energy and the associated

concentrated solar power (CSP) plants may be divided into four variants: parabolic trough (PT), Fresnel reflector (FR), solar tower (ST) and solar dish (SD). CSP plants are a very promising option for use in the Sun Belt.[185]

The exploitation of solar energy is rapidly growing in the MENA region due to its significant potential. Almost all countries use PV to meet part of their electricity demand. The United Arab Emirates is the leader in the region with 22.5 MW of installed capacity, followed by Egypt, Mauritania and Morocco with approximately 15 MW each, and Algeria, Bahrain, Libya and Saudi Arabia using approximately 5 MW. It must be noted that the reported values for solar PV are notably underestimated due to its decentralized characteristics which makes it difficult to report on and account for CSP will also contribute to the region's growing share of solar energy. With the largest concentration CSP use in Algeria, Egypt and Morocco, the Arab region accounted for 30 per cent of global CSP plant operations in 2011. In 2013, the United Arab Emirates also became a major player in the CSP market when Shams 1, one of the world's largest CSP plants, with an installed capacity of 100 MW, became operational.[186] Algeria, Morocco, Saudi Arabia, and the United Arab Emirates also have significant plans to increase the exploitation of solar energy.

(a) Water use requirement

Thermoelectric power plants produce 90 per cent of electricity worldwide, including in Arab countries. Thermoelectric plants utilize varying amounts of water, depending on the cooling technology used. The use of water has two major components, namely, water extraction-release and consumption, the latter being the water lost to evaporation. Water in the extraction-release component, although not lost, has important implications on the environment, including stress on the aquifer and, in the case of water extracted from rivers, lakes and seas, the reduction of available environmental flows and the warming of the aquatic environment as the water is released. The significance of the water-use component depends largely on local environmental factors, including available water sources and aquatic life. The three main types of cooling systems, namely, once through cooling, wet recirculation cooling and dry cooling systems, each have advantages and disadvantages in terms of water withdrawal, consumption, capital costs, plant efficiency, and ecological impact, as illustrated in table 1.[187]

Table 1. Types of cooling systems: advantages and disadvantages

Cooling type	Water withdrawal	Water consumption	Capital cost	Plant efficiency	Ecological impact
Once through cooling	Intense	Moderate	Low	Most efficient	Intense
Wet cooling	Moderate	Intense	Moderate	Efficient	Moderate
Dry cooling	None	None	High	Less efficient	Low

Source: Based on United States Department of Energy, 2009.

Table 2. Comparison of consumptive water use of various power plant technologies using various cooling methods

Technology	Cooling technology	Consumptive water use (m³/MWh)	Performance penalty[a] (percentage)	Cost penalty[b] (percentage)
Coal/nuclear	Once through cooling	87-102[c]		
	Recirculating cooling	1.5-2.8		
	Dry cooling	0.19-0.25		
Natural gas	Recirculating cooling	0.76		
Power tower	Recirculating cooling	1.9-2.8		
	Combination hybrid parallel cooling	0.34-0.95	1-3	5
	Dry cooling	0.34	1.3	
Parabolic trough	Recirculating cooling	3		
	Combination hybrid parallel cooling	0.38-1.7	1-4	8
	Dry cooling	0.3	4.5-5	2-9
Dish/engine	Mirror washing cooling	0.08		
Fresnel	Recirculating cooling	3.8		

Source: United States Department of Energy, 2009.
Notes: a. Performance penalty is the annual energy output loss relative to the most efficient cooling technique.
b. Cost penalty is the added cost to produce the electricity.
c. Majority of this amount is returned to the source, but at an elevated temperature.

62

The required water volume for the cooling of nuclear power plants largely depends on the technology chosen, with no specific example of dry cooling for a large nuclear plant. Other water uses include liquid waste dilution. CSP plants also require water for cooling systems and for cleaning mirrors and lenses, which may be a challenge in water-scarce areas. With regard to efficient and sustainable water use, CSP plants based on dry cooling system are preferable. Typically, such plants are approximately 10 per cent more expensive than their water-cooled counterparts,[188] as illustrated in table 2.

Many power plants use freshwater for cooling. However, waste water and salt water offer alternative possibilities, with both advantages and disadvantages. Obviously, sea water is abundant for coastal power plants, but warming the local aquatic environment remains a challenge. The effects of water discharge on the environment in terms of biodiversity, aquatic fauna and flora must be weighed quite carefully.

(b) Land use

Energy options are site-dependent and restricted to certain locations or resource areas. Nuclear power provides concentrated power generation with small land use but with high security and environmental constraints. Several factors impact land use, including cooling technologies, tracking systems for solar cells and energy storage. With regard to the physical land requirement of actual energy generation, solar plants are comparably more land-intensive than nuclear power plants. As concerns nuclear energy, a minimum land area of approximately 0.3 km² is required for a nuclear plant of approximately 1000 MW capacity, with an additional 0.1 km² required if a cooling tower is used. Solar energy plants require

approximately 30 times more land than nuclear energy plants. In terms of energy, a nuclear power plant is able to generate base load power for an annual duration of 7500 to 8000 hours. In contrast, a solar power plant without storage can at best generate energy at full power for approximately 2000 equivalent hours per year.

Water use and land requirements are not the only factors for the evaluation of energy sources. Other factors include environmental impacts and socioeconomic factors such as human capacity, infrastructure development, health risks, economic opportunities, and technological limitations. For example, the safety of nuclear power plants is of paramount importance not only on a national but also on a regional scale and is tied to both normal operations and emergency situations, not disregarding the processing of the used fuel and the generated waste. Human resources are another important factor that should be evaluated in order to determine availability of specific competencies to support the sector's development requirements. The ability of local, national and regional industries to benefit and create jobs in relationship to the selected energy technologies is an important factor that tends to incite much-needed private-sector participation. Technological limitations are an important factor to consider for the success of the selected technology, as is the case for solar power and its limitations of supply intermittency, storage capacity and its compatibility with existing grids. Solar potential and intermittency strongly call for regional cooperation with interconnection of transmission grids to allow the balance of supply and demand between regions or countries. Table 3 presents some of the above criteria in a qualitative comparison for nuclear, CSP and PV power generation technologies.

Table 3. Solar and nuclear energy: qualitative comparative analysis

		Cost competitiveness		Water requirements	Land use	Environmental impact and long-term sustainability	Socioeconomic co-effects		Human resources and training
		LCOE[a]	Balancing costs[b]				Job creation	Local manufacturing potential	
Nuclear Energy		+ +[c]	+	One trough cooling: - - Wet cooling tower: - Dry cooling tower: +	+ +	- -[d]	+	+	+
Solar energy	CSP (PT, SD, ST)	+[e]	-	+	- -	+	-	+ +	-
	PV	+ +[32]	- -	+ +	-	+	-		- -[f]

Sources: Cour de Comptes, 2014; Fraunhofer Institut for Solar Energy System ISE, 2013; authors.

Notes:
a. LCOE stands for "levelized cost of electricity".
b. Balancing costs contains the grid optimization costs to make up intermittencies or storage technologies installation.
c. Information taken from Cour des Comptes, 2014.
d. For example, nuclear waste management is an important issue to consider in terms of the long-term sustainability and environmental impact of this energy source.
e. Information taken from Fraunhofer Institut for Solar Energy System ISE, 2013.
f. Most parts of the PV value chain are cheaper abroad; consequently, the value in term of human resources and training is very poor for the country.

3. Cogeneration and desalination

A large portion of the energy consumed in the GCC countries, and a smaller portion in other countries in the region, is dedicated to desalination in order to meet the growing water demand, with the GCC countries producing more than half of the world's desalinated water.[189] Some projections claim that most of the water needed in the oil production in Arab countries could be gained through desalination in the near future if the water demand continues to increase at the current rates. Kuwait, for example, is expected to consume energy equivalent to the oil production quota before the year 2040, with approximately 70 per cent to be used for electricity production and desalination.[190]

In fact, more and more countries from the region will also be concerned by this energy-intensive mode of producing fresh water since, according to some estimates, water demand is expected to be five times higher by 2050. Currently already, the region's water demand exceeds natural water supplies by almost 20 per cent.[191]

Several technology options may be used in desalination processes, which include the following three main types:

- Thermal desalination based on destillation: These options, mainly multi-stage flash (MSF) and multi- effect desalination (MED), are capable of using low-grade heat from power plants, and are widely used in countries of the GCC in cogenerating plants that produce both electricity and desalinate water by burning fossil fuels or natural gas. In the case of both MSF and MED, heat is required at 70-130°C[192] and the process requires 25[193]-100 kWh[194] of thermal energy per cubic meter of water. A newer generation of this technology is the MED mechanical vapour compressor, which is reported to use only 10 kWh/m³.[195, 196] However, it is very important to optimize the thermodynamic cycles and operation of such plants, taking into account the time of day and seasonal variation of electrical demand and proper sizing of water storage buffers, in order to improve their overall efficiencies and maximize the part of energy used for desalination that relies on the recovery of wasted heat from the power generation process;
- Electricity and desalination: Using electrical energy to power a reverse osmosis (RO) process or an electrodialysis process is the most widely used desalination technology worldwide, including in most non-GCC countries in the Arab region. It requires 4-6 kWh of electricity per cubic metre of water,[197] depending on the salt content of the water source and the desired salinity of the produced fresh water. The operation of electricity-based desalination plants can also be optimized by taking into account the time of day and seasonal variation of the demand curve for electricity, and sizing water storage buffers properly, in order to operate to the highest extent possible during the base load part of the curve, where the produced electricity is the most efficient;
- Combined electricity and thermal-based options: These processes include thermal vapour compression (TVC) or a combination of a thermal process with an electric one in the same desalination plant, such as an MSF-RO hybrid plant using the best features of each technology to match the desired salinity of the produced fresh water to that of the water source.

Forward osmosis (FO) technologies are also being tested as an alternative to reverse osmosis desalination, which offer the potential of increased energy savings. The technology uses biomimetic membranes[198] to desalinate brackish water or seawater using less pressure. While its commercial viability remains to be seen with testing underway in Oman, original research on FO proposed it for use in emergency conditions, such as to reduce the weight of storing more food and potable water in lifeboats.[199]

Improving the efficiency of desalination processes can be achieved by closely monitoring the energy use in existing facilities and subsequently retrofitting them accordingly.

Technological choices for future desalination plants should be considered based on a holistic approach that examines the following: (a) the nature of the water source and its location; (b) the type and source of energy needed to operate the technology; (c) the desired quality of the water required; and (d) the resulting brine stream and environmental impacts associated with the technological application in a specific location.

A wide range of renewable energy solutions are currently being proposed for use in desalination. These vary from rudimentary individual and small systems, mainly for remote and rural areas, to sophisticated centralized systems using conventional desalination technologies.

Finally, desalination activities have important environmental impacts that include emissions of carbondioxid (CO_2) and air pollutants, when fossil fuels constitute the primary energy source, and the disposal of the highly concentrated brine that is produced during the thermal and desalination process. It must be noted that the brine produced per unit of generated fresh water from thermal distillation is much more significant than that generated from RO.[200]

4. Produced water

The extraction, production and refining of oil and gas require significant quantities of water. Much of the water used in the extraction process is recaptured along with the produced oil, generating a major waste stream that poses a challenge in terms of treatment and disposal. The interlinkage between water and energy is particularly striking in the water-scarce Arab region. Some GCC countries rely on non-renewable groundwater and desalination to meet the water demands of the energy sector. Saudi Arabia uses nearly 106 m3 of desalinated water, which is then transported over 300-400 km to be utilized in the Ghawar oilfield.[201] Water is also used in several stages of oil extraction from drilling wells, hydraulic fracturing, well completion and treatment to secondary recovery and various processes for improving the efficiency of oil displacement and extraction, such as water flooding and enhanced oil recovery.

The increasing energy demand is being met through the exploration of more difficult environments, increasing the recovery factors of mature fields, and production of oil and gas from unconventional sources such as tar sands and shale gas. Improving recovery factors in more mature oil fields and tapping unconventional sources require more water than conventional exploration. The lack of surface water sources in the Arab region mandates that water demand is met through two primary sources, namely, groundwater and desalination; ironically, both of these sources are energy-intense.

It is estimated to take 16.7 to 46 litres of water per barrel of extracted oil, which includes the water needed for drilling, flooding and treating; drilling alone requires approximately 12.6 litres of water per barrel of oil equivalent.[202] The amount of water required for refining processes is also significant, even though technological advances made it possible in the 1980s to decrease demand from several cubic metres of water to the current requirement of 200 to 800 litres of water per ton of crude oil.[203] Gas extraction, in general, is less water intense but site-specific, depending on geological formations, and can even vary from well to well within the same well field. Of greater concern than the quantity of water used in gas extraction is the quality of water associated with fracking and the associated chemicals injected to ensure optimal hydraulic fracturing. Given the chronic water scarcity of the region, the water requirement is a major challenge to the continued development of the Arab region's large hydrocarbon endowments.

This challenge is only increased when considering the volume of produced water associated with oil and gas extraction. The worldwide estimate for produced water is three barrels of water for every barrel of oil produced, which is predicted to increase at varying estimates of 1.7[204] to10[205] per cent per year. Ratios of produced water-to-oil vary greatly between countries and oil fields in the region. Oman has the highest water-oil ratio of between 6:1[206] and 10:1[207] and the United Arab Emirates the lowest of 0.35:1.[208] The produced water is normally contaminated and is traditionally dealt with through energy-intensive and costly approaches by either deep injection into suitable rock formations or treatment to remove contaminants.

The water-energy nexus has pushed oil companies towards using innovative technologies to lower the volume of produced water for oil production. Technology advances include increased use of horizontal wells, zonal isolation, injection pressure control in fracturing, converting produced wastewater to value,[209] and using solar energy for steam generation and injection into reservoirs as part of enhanced oil recovery.

Conversion of produced wastewater to a valuable commodity is particularly interesting within the WEF nexus security framework for the Arab region. A pilot study was undertaken in Oman, where new water treatment techniques using reed beds in the Nimr oil field were used to treat the produced wastewater, and subsequently to irrigate biosaline agriculture plants.[210] Operational costs, compared to deep water disposal costs, proved to be competitive and a promising alternative to current options.[211] Nevertheless, the feasibility of such treatment and reuse is subject to the quality of the water produced, which varies from one oil field to another and in some cases between wells in the same well field. This cost varies greatly and ranges from less than $0.01 per barrel to more than $5.00 per barrel.[212] Certain factors, including salinity and heavy metals, end use and expected revenue return, treatment requirements and cost, and long-term consistency of produced water volume, need to be considered within a water-energy nexus when assessing available water-energy synergies, environmental benefits and economic feasibility. Solutions for produced water need to be multidisciplinary, matching produced water quality and treatment and energy demand to the needs of various end users.

The treatment and further reuse of produced water beyond the oil sector may be part of the solution to water scarcity in the Arab region. However, the produced water quality and quantity specificities of each country, and each well field, need to be assessed carefully within a water- energy nexus framework. The Oman pilot study of the Nimr oil field with the highest produced water-to-oil ratio of 6:1 is specific to Oman and the actual water quality of this particular oil field. The volume of produced water is generally unmatched in other countries in the GCC region, such as Kuwait and Saudi Arabia, where the water-to-oil ratio is 2.4:1 and 0.73:1, respectively.[213] In countries with low volumes of produced water, the use of treated produced water beyond the oil sector is most likely unfeasible, as primary uses of any treated water will be to meet the oil sector's own demands. Another barrier is the availability of low quality water from alternative sources such as municipal waste water or even seawater, which, in many cases, is less costly to treat and more strategically located in proximity to potential end users.

The mere reliance on the technological advances in the oil industries and its will to spend more on research and development to manage used and produced water is insufficient. Policy makers need to create an environment that facilitates nexus analysis through all stages of oil exploration involving the reduction of water use, especially of fresh water, that further encourages reuse, makes environmental standards more stringent in terms of disposal, and demands the development of alternative uses of treated produced water by the oil industry.

C. Technology options for improved water-energy-food security

1. Energy use in the delivery of water services

The delivery of water services is energy-intensive along the entire water chain. The intensity of energy use differs with varying sources of water, the treatment technologies required and utilized, the horizontal distance of the source to the end use, the vertical elevation differences, and wastewater treatment levels and technologies utilized.

The major water sources in the region are surface water, groundwater and desalinated water. Surface water normally requires the least amount of energy as these systems generally depend on gravity. Groundwater abstraction is more energy-intensive and depends largely on local conditions, such as depth and well efficiency with a range of energy needed for the pumping of 0.31 to 0.79 kWh to lift $1m^3$ a vertical distance of 100 m as analysed from pumping stations in the California State Water Project.[214] ESCWA calculates that approximately 0.36 kWh is needed to lift $1m^3$ of groundwater a vertical distance of 100 m while only 0.04kWh is needed to pump $1m^3$ of surface water a horizontal distance of 100km.[215] However, these energy requirements fail to account for the energy required for water treatment, which is normally considered minimal for fresh groundwater, with only chlorine dosing required, and slightly higher for surface water at approximately 0.3 kWh/m^3.[216] This figure varies locally depending on water quality. The most energy-intense process is desalination, with varying energy consumption depending on the technology used as illustrated in table 4.

The above energy requirement listing for water production leads to the grouping of Arab countries based on the energy intensity needed for water production. This grouping is based on water withdrawal by source, which is closely related to energy demand and not necessary to available water sources (map 6).

Table 4. Energy used in selected desalination technologies

Seawater desalination technology	Electrical energy use (KWh/m³)	Thermal energy – stand-alone (MJ/m³)	Thermal energy – cogeneration (MJ/m³)
Reverse osmosis (brackish)	0.5-2.5	None	None
Reverse osmosis (sea)	5-9	None	None
Multi-effect distillation	1.5-2.5	150-220	100
Multi-stage flash	3.5-5	250-300	160-170

Source: ESCWA, 2009b.

Three groups can be identified based on abstraction by water sources and energy required as follows:

- High-energy demand: This category includes countries that depend primarily on groundwater and desalination while surface water use is not significant. This category would include the GCC countries, which have a high energy demand for water production, such as Bahrain, where desalination alone accounts for 30 per cent of total energy use,[217] while in Libya and Saudi Arabia, groundwater pumping accounts for 14 per cent and 10 per cent, respectively, of the total fuel consumption in the country;[218]
- Medium-energy demand: This category includes countries that depend on a mix of sources, with surface water constituting an appreciable portion but groundwater being the dominant source of abstraction. Typical countries in this category include Jordan, Lebanon, Tunisia, and Yemen. The Jordanian water sector consumes about 14 per cent of the total annual electricity generated;[219]
- Low-energy demand: This category is for countries that largely depend on surface water and includes countries such as Egypt and the Syrian Arab Republic.

The region's energy demand is further complicated by diminishing resources and increased urbanization, and long transfer distances of water from coastal desalination plants or well fields to cities far away. The Disi-Amman water conveyance project pumps water over 325 km, with a total energy requirement of 2 per cent of Jordan's annual energy consumption, including the groundwater pumping component.[220]

Unaccounted-for water loss in the networks in the region, which ranges between 15 per cent and 60 per cent,[221] constitutes an additional energy demand and an additional economic cost, which is normally not transferred to the consumer in the region. This is where the benefits of water demand side management do not only reflect on the water saved but also on the associated virtual energy savings incurred from providing the saved water.

Downstream of the water chain, there is an energy demand for wastewater treatment and discharge, which varies greatly according to the level of treatment and technology used. Primary treatment has an energy requirement range of 0.1 to 0.3 KWh/m³, whereas secondary treatment has a range of 0.27 to 0.59 kWh/m³.[222]

Map 6. Water sources in selected Arab countries

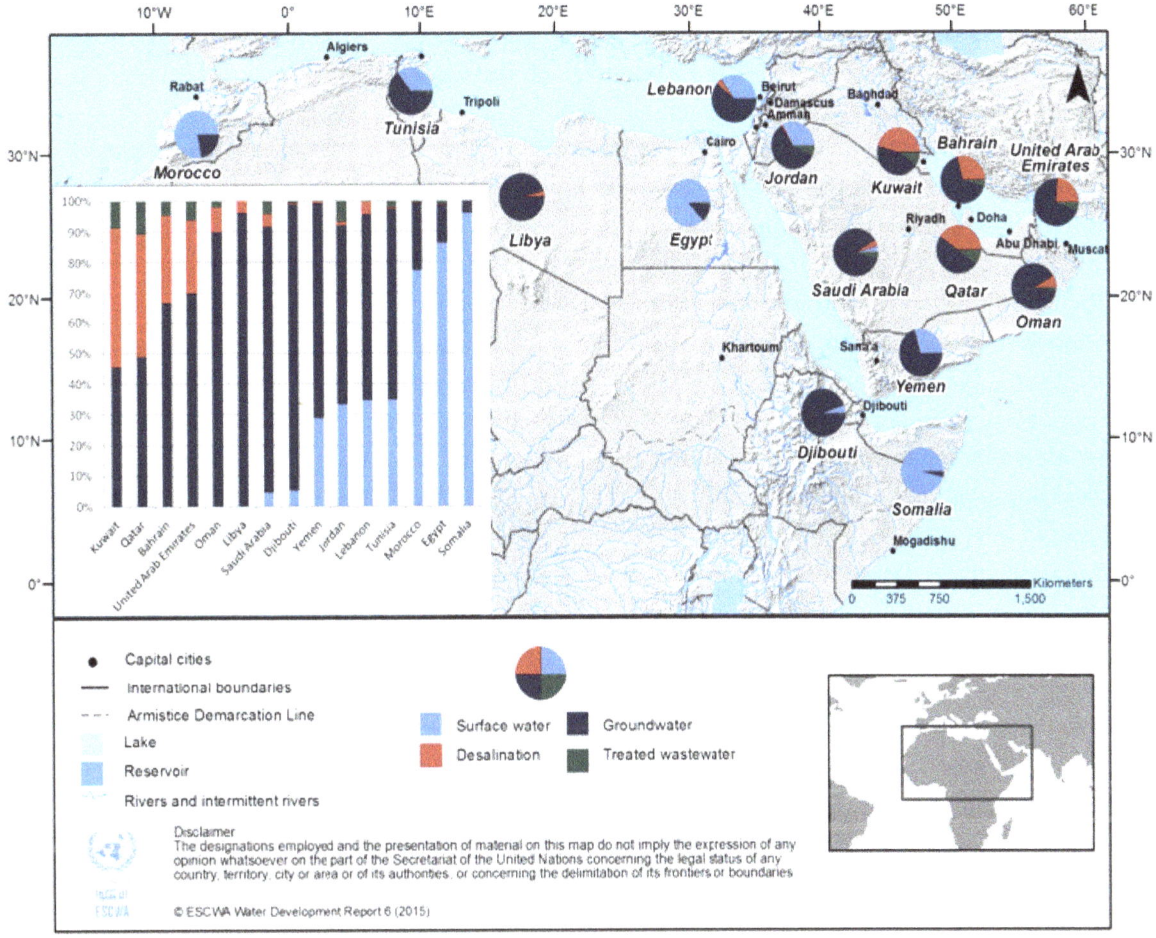

Source: FAO, n.d.a.

Note: Not all data are for the same year. Surface water withdrawal for Egypt was calculated based on the difference between total freshwater withdrawal and groundwater withdrawal.

This energy range is lower than that required for desalination, which should serve as an incentive for countries relying on desalination to increase utilization of treated wastewater at a lower energy cost and lower environmental impacts on the marine environment.

Intermittency of water service

The delivery of water service in several countries of the region, such as Jordan, Lebanon, Palestine, Syrian Arab Republic, and Yemen, may not be on a continuous basis due to several reasons, including water shortages, economic hardship, armed conflicts, and more commonly due to power shortages. Intermittent supply carries with it several complications at the service-provider and consumer level. At the level of the service provider, intermittent supply results in increased maintenance costs as networks are alternately exposed to water and air and variations in pressure. This leads to higher corrosion and pipe burst and thus to higher leakage, which carries a multitude of economic losses in the water lost and the associated energy used to produce this water, in the repair cost, in malfunctioning of water meters, and the lost consumer confidence in the water service which leads to a lower willingness to pay. This, in turn, translates into lower income for the service provider and a lower capability to invest and improve the network resulting in a vicious cycle of poorer networks.

For domestic use, intermittent supply has potential health and economic implications. Irregular water supplies result in negative pressure in the network allowing for external contaminants to be sucked into the network through cracks and joints. Furthermore, static water conditions can also lead to microbial growth. Intermittent water supply further impacts consumers who are forced to employ additional water storage space often in non-food grade containers, leading some consumers to turn to additional water treatment processes in order to maintain quality or purchase bottled water. Such measures come at a cost and affect the poor the greatest, forcing them in some instances into unhealthy alternatives.

Intermittent supply also has negative economic and health impacts for the agriculture sector. Economically, it means having to either apply water at suboptimal periods of the day or overwater due to the inconvenient scheduling of water supplies, which results in low-efficiency farming. Farmers often offset this through either constructing costly on-farm storage or locating an alternative source, such as groundwater pumping with its associated costs of well construction and pumping operations. Farmers

without economic means resort to the use of untreated waste water, which has associated health risks to both the farmer and the end consumer.

2. Energy use in the agricultural sector: implications for groundwater consumption

(a) Energy requirements for pumping groundwater

Considerable technological advances in groundwater use for irrigation have led to increased food production. This led Saudi Arabia to become self-sufficient in wheat production and even led to the country exporting wheat in the early 1990s, which was also made possible through the subsidy of energy, technology and wheat prices. This development resulted in the mining of non-renewable groundwater resources at unsustainable rates, leading to a drop in the water table and a decrease in water quality. Globally, most groundwater mining occurs in West Asia and North Africa, with Libya and Saudi Arabia accounting for approximately 77 per cent of the extraction of non-renewable water resources.[223]

The agricultural sector is a major consumer of energy, which is largely destined for the operation of pumps. Libya devotes 14 per cent of its total fuel consumption to groundwater pumping and Saudi Arabia approximately 5 per cent of its total electricity consumption.[224] Increasingly, groundwater is mined from deep aquifers, for instance at depths of more than 250 m around Riyadh. In other places, water is pumped over long distances, for instance 325 km between the Disi Aquifer and Amman. It is estimated that most countries in the region rely on groundwater for approximately 50 per cent of their water supply, reaching as high as 84 per cent for countries on the Arabian Peninsula.[225]

Due to subsidies being provided for their acquisition and operation, water pumps have proliferated in the region and resulted in wasteful water practices. Ground water abstraction is largely dependent on the availability of subsidized energy, and Governments had the ability to control the amount of abstracted water by re-allocating these subsidies. With the introduction of pumps relying on renewable energy, this would be no longer the case. Solar and wind pumps include economical features that are very attractive to farmers, and their increased proliferation might lead to extensive ground water abstraction, which would be particularly disastrous in water-scarce environments such as the Arab region.[226]

The Ministry of Agriculture in Yemen has cooperated with the Co-operative and Agricultural Credit Bank to introduce solar-powered pumps. This allows farmers to become more competitive as current fuel costs, which are already subsidized, represent approximately 60 per cent of the total cost of agricultural production.[227]

Most water users in the Arab region have unrestricted access rights to groundwater resources, which is seen as a common-pool resource dilemma. This mindset is leading to the so-called tragedy of the commons[228] wherein individual groundwater users have little or no incentive to conserve the water. Without proper legislation that sets limits and rules on the pumping of groundwater, there will be no economic or policy restraints to water abstraction unless appropriate ways of setting a fair charge or a perception of increasing groundwater scarcity are introduced. One way to regulate the overabstraction of water in the absence of a fair water charge is through the control of energy use, which would be impossible in the case of privately-owned pumps operating or relying on solar or wind energy.[229]

(b) Energy requirements for cold storage, trade and transfer of fresh produce

The use of energy in agriculture can be further divided into direct and indirect uses. Direct uses encompass the energy consumed through actual agricultural operations, and indirect uses include the energy used in energy-intensive inputs such as fertilizers and pesticides. The share between direct and indirect energy use in middle- and high-income countries is 60 per cent and 40 per cent, respectively, with the share of direct energy consumption lower in low-income countries as most food is consumed fresh.[230]

Food production consumes energy both prior to, during and after farming. Prior to farming is the production and distribution of fertilizers and other inputs in which energy is a major component. During farming, energy is consumed in direct agricultural activities such as tilling, planting, irrigating, and harvesting. After farming, energy is consumed during the entire process of transportation, storage, processing, and retailing. In order to maintain their quality, agricultural products are stored either dried or cooled, both of which can be energy-intensive and which, according to FAO estimates, can account up to 10 per cent of the total carbon footprint for certain products.[231] Without drying or cooling, food losses are substantially high, including the loss of the water and energy embedded into the food or waste. The energy embedded in global annual food losses can reach up to 38 per cent of the total energy used in the entire food value chain. The percentage can be even higher for water since most of the water is consumed during the production stage.[232]

In light of the challenges caused by increasing water scarcity resulting from climate change, the need to reallocate water from agriculture to other sectors will increase, as will the need to use water more efficiently and productively. The region will thus move towards more virtual water trade, whereby it will import the water that is actually embedded in the food acquired from overseas markets. The water that would have been used to produce food locally can be reallocated to other ways of usage where it can be used more efficiently. This will considerably reduce the levels of energy consumption for the concerned crops up to the point of import.[233] However, the pursuit of food self-sufficiency under the notion of food security by many Arab countries still affects such rellocations considerably.

IV. Water and Energy for Food Security

This chapter explores the interlinkages between food security and the water and energy sectors from a nexus perspective. It discusses the dependency of the agriculture sector on the limited water resources in the Arab region along with the high energy requirements needed for water pumping and fertilizer production. It further reviews available technological options in the agriculture sector and focuses on how efficiency improvements can lead to increased water and energy security. It finally examines the concept of virtual water trade and investments abroad in relation to increased food security.

A. Overview

1. Food security from a nexus perspective

Food security is said to exist "when all people, at all times, have physical, social and economic access to sufficient, safe and nutritious food, which meets their dietary needs and food preferences for an active and healthy life".[234] Defined as such, food security has four main dimensions, namely: having sufficient food in quantitative and qualitative terms; being able to access and afford food; using food appropriately and benefiting from nutritious foods; and ensuring year-round availability. Whenever one of these dimensions is not met, the concerned population group or individual is said to face food insecurity.

Food security is often confused with food self-sufficiency. However, the two concepts are quite different from each another, as is explained as follows:

- Food self-sufficiency is premised within a closed economic system whereby a country seeks to meet the largest share of its food needs possible through local production. This approach was common in agrarian societies and developing countries during the 1960s and 1970s when countries sought to be self-sufficient in several strategic economic sectors due to political exigencies and mistrust of the international trading system, which was prevalent during this period;
- Food security calls for a more open economic approach where food deficits may be offset through international trade. This approach is a result of natural resource constraints and changing production and consumption patterns, based on the understanding that alternative measures are needed to satisfy national food needs across the four dimensions of food security. Investments in commodity futures and foreign lands are an essential part of food security strategies in what has become an increasingly globalized and economically interdependent world. This is complemented by discussions regarding the water rights and access to the energy needed to ensure food security through domestic production or trade.

There is also a growing grassroots movement promoting the concept of food sovereignty, which embodies the right of communities, peoples and States to determine their own food and agricultural policies with respect to providing food for people and espousing the values of food providers through local food systems and respect for the environment.[235] An Arab Network for Food Sovereignty has been recently established in support of this movement.[236] The emergence of this new concept highlights the importance of considering which types of sustainable agriculture schemes, rural livelihoods programmes and trade policies should be pursued in order to guarantee food security for urban and rural populations across the region given changing regional dynamics.

Rapid population growth, improving living standards, migration patterns, and rapid dietary changes since the 1960s have altered the quantity and pattern of food demand in the Arab region. During the 1970s, political concerns led Arab countries to pursue food self-sufficiency policies and expand agricultural production in order to avoid dependency on foreign markets. The agricultural sector was, in turn, largely subsidized to encourage domestic production, to the detriment of sustainable land and water resources policies. However, increasing water scarcity, land degradation policies and associated growth in demand have revealed that the region is unable to meet its food needs at the national or regional levels. The anticipated negative impacts of climate change, drought and desertification further prevent countries to significantly enhance their food self-sufficiency despite efforts aimed at increasing agricultural productivity.

However, the recent price volatility in food markets, which lead to a string of food export restrictions, has once again raised concerns regarding the region's reliance on external food markets. This has led to calls for increasing food self-sufficiency, if not at national levels then at least at the regional level, by enhancing agriculture production in Arab countries with a comparative advantage in land and water resources, such as the Sudan, setting up food storage facilities and pursuing agricultural land investments abroad.

2. Reliable access to water and energy resources indispensible for food security

A steady supply of water and energy is needed for food production, transport, storage and/or handling, processing, cooking, food safety, and shock avoidance. As such, water and energy are inextricably linked to food security and more so in the water-scarce Arab region where the economic structure is overly dependent on energy resources. Increasing water scarcity has decimated many communities or made them overreliant on aquifer pumping, which has led to dramatic falls of groundwater tables and the deterioration of water quality in some cases. For instance, the aquifer around Riyadh fell by approximately 100 metres between the 1980s and 2000s due to the heavy water abstraction for urban and agricultural uses.[237] Agriculture water use is thus firmly entrenched in food security, social justice and public policy concerns, as agriculture's low contribution to the GDP, the persistence of low water-use efficiency in agriculture and low agricultural productivity render it difficult to economically justify the expansion of the agricultural sector in the light of water scarcity.[238]

The rapid industrialization and urbanization of the region combined with intensified globalization have lead to the procurement and consumption of food becoming more energy intensive. Without steady, reliable and affordable supply of energy, food loss will increase, which translates into the loss of water and energy that is embedded in the production process. The region is also rapidly moving towards unsustainable levels of production and consumption as displayed by the increasingly high consumption footprint, particularly in the GCC countries. The achievement of food security in the region will remain strongly linked to the availability and steady supply of water and energy, and appropriate policies, good incentives and a proper institutional framework will be needed to better address the issue within a nexus analytical framework.

3. Agricultural sector as major consumer of freshwater available in the Arab region

Agriculture is one of the economic sectors most heavily dependent on water availability. However, the overabundance of water, in the form of floods, for instance, has a dramatic effect on the production, supply and quality of agricultural produce and ultimately on the well-being of the population and the economic stability of the country. Globally, the agricultural sector consumes 80 per cent and more of the freshwater that is available in most countries, including the Arab region. The remaining water is used in the more water-use efficient and productive domestic and industrial sectors.[239] Given this discrepancy, many are increasingly calling for Arab countries to reallocate more of their water to the domestic and industrial sectors, as the contribution of agriculture to

national revenue is less significant.[240] However, such a decision would have vast political, economic and social ramifications for agriculture-producing countries as its impact would leave millions of unskilled labourers without any economic means for survival.

According to the World Bank, 85 per cent of water withdrawal in the region is used for irrigation.[241] However, average water-use efficiency in regional irrigation systems stands at approximately 50-60 per cent compared to well over 80 per cent in Australia or the arid south-western United States. One of the reasons for the Arab region's low efficiency rates could be the choice of crops. Growing cereals and other field crops favoured in the region, and using land as pasture are less efficient than growing fruits and vegetables. Irrigation by sprinkler and surface irrigation, as is utilized for field crops records high losses of water caused by evapotranspiration as compared to drop irrigation that is used for the cultivation of fruits and vegetables. It is estimated that water productivity in the MENA region stands at only $0.26/m^3$ compared to $0.65/m^3$ globally.[242] In addressing the challenges of rising water scarcity, enhancing the overall efficiency of irrigation systems and water allocation should be the driving force of regional water policies and strategies.

4. Human right to food

The right to food is enshrined in the Universal Declaration of Human Rights[243] and the International Covenant on the Economic, Social and Cultural Rights,[244] which were accepted well before the human right to water, sanitation or sustainable energy was articulated by the global community. Interestingly, Article 11 of the International Covenant also recognizes the fundamental right of everyone to be free from hunger, "taking into account the problems of both food-importing and food-exporting countries, to ensure an equitable distribution of world food supplies in relation to need". This supports the need to incorporate trade in discussions related to the right to food in nexus analytical frameworks related to the Arab region, given that the region is heavily dependent on food imports.

While the right to food aims to ensure that food is available, accessible and adequate to every human being, this concept is not equivalent to food security. Food security is neither an obligation nor an entitlement to food, but rather a prerequisite to ensure the right to food for all. However, as a human right, the right to food within a nexus construct cannot be achieved in the absences of other human rights, such as the right to water and development, as these are prerequisites for agricultural production, food preparation, human health, and hygiene.

The right to food is closely linked to poverty, which is a state of permanent or sustained deprivations of one resource or more that prohibits the enjoyment of a good standard of living.[245] The vast majority of poor people in the Arab region are marginalized rural and urban dwellers, the proportion of which has remained relatively constant at approximately 20 per cent of the population, increasing slightly with the onset of the social upheavals that have swept across the region since 2012. The number of undernourished people has also increased from approximately 30 million in the early 1990s to approximately 50 million by 2011 with countries experiencing upheavals and higher levels of undernourishment.[246]

As a marginalized group, women are particularly concerned with the right to adequate food as they are among the most affected by food insecurity largely due to a lack of access to alternate means of income other than from agriculture. Women's share in non-agricultural employment stands at less than 20 per cent in the region compared to a worldwide average of approximately 40 per cent.[247] This is further exacerbated by the current sociopolitical disruptions and conflicts in many countries and the prevalence of discriminatory laws and traditions. In rural areas and in poor urban environments, women also lack adequate access to reliable supplies of water and energy. Addressing the nexus from a human rights approach that draws upon CEDAW Article 14 would benefit rural Arab women who struggle in difficult environments that undermine their fundamental rights, including those to adequate food and water and access to energy.[248, 249]

In pursuing the human right to food, tools and guidelines are available to Arab countries to improve food security at the national level. For example, FAO prepared the Voluntary guidelines to support the progressive realization of the right to adequate food in the context of national food security.[250] While the document fails to mainstream the interlinkages between food and water, Guideline 8C explicitly refers to water resources by stating that since "access to water in sufficient quantity and quality for all is fundamental for life and health, States should strive to improve access to, and promote sustainable use of, water resources and their allocation among users giving due regard to efficiency and the satisfaction of basic human needs in an equitable manner and that balances the requirement of preserving or restoring the functioning of ecosystems with domestic, industrial and agricultural needs, including safeguarding drinking-water quality".[251] However, in calling for the satisfaction of basic human needs when referring to the water resources, the FAO approach prioritizes the right to food and avoids adopting a human rights-based approach to ensure the human rights to food and water in a universal and indivisible manner.

B. Production and use of fertilizers for agriculture

1. Fertilizers for food security

Mineral fertilizers are among the major factors behind the rapid growth in global cereal production that started in the 1960s, which led to the Green Revolution.[252] This trend is not expected to abate in the Arab region in the foreseeable future since most countries are still aiming for a level of self-sufficiency, at least for such selected products as fruits and vegetables.[253, 254] The continued use of fertilizers for food production will be necessary in order to keep pace with the growing world population that is expected to reach nine billion by 2050.[255]

2. Fertilizers and energy linkages

The processing of mineral or inorganic fertilizers is energy-intensive. Nitrogen (N) fertilizer production, which is produced by capturing nitrogen from the air or in urea using a complex chemical reaction, is among the most energy-

intensive. Phosphate (P) and potassium (K) are mined and then processed into phosphate and potassium fertilizers for use in agriculture individually or, in most cases, as NPK complex. Once processed, they have to be transported over long distances as only a handful of countries are able to produce these fertilizers economically: about 70 per cent of the world phosphate is produced in only three countries while 80 per cent of the potassium produced worldwide is involved in international trade.[256, 257]

It is estimated that the consumption of energy represents about 70 per cent of the cost of manufacturing fertilizers. As such, the energy price is transmitted into the price of fertilizers, with volatile energy prices heavily affecting farmers' revenues. However, price transmission is not always a given as observed through the recent drop in oil prices, which failed to lead to a decrease in fertilizer prices. This discrepancy arises not only because of the increased global demand for fertilizers but also due to the lack of an increase in production capacity following a decrease in energy prices, as the construction of fertilizer plants is costly, difficult and time-consuming.[258]

3. Agricultural run-off and effects on water quality

The use of fertilizers can lead to undesirable environmental effects, especially when misused. One of the best-known negative effects is the contamination of such water resources as rivers and aquifers by water run-off and infiltration. Nitrogen fertilizers are easily transformed into nitrates, which are water-soluble and thus easily contaminate water resources. Nitrates are not easily degradable and remain in soil and water for long periods of time. Their harmful effects are further enhanced when compounded with certain pesticides. Urea, for instance, produces harmful ammonia and nitrous oxide emanations, which may lead to both surface and ground water resources contamination.[259, 260]

The discharge of fertilizers and nutrients into water bodies may lead to an increased growth of such aquatic plants as algae, which could reduce oxygen levels and consequently affect aquatic life and, therefore, impede economic activities. The excess use of organic fertilizers, especially manure and human excreta, may also

lead to serious environmental degradation, including water pollution and the acidification of land and water.[261]

Despite not being considered a major agricultural area of the world, Arab countries are nevertheless major consumers of manufactured fertilizers (figure 11).

This overuse of agricultural chemicals has often led to water and land pollution and is one of the causes of land and water quality degradation, as has been the case in the Nile Delta or in Palestine.

Figure 11. NPK fertilizer consumption per hectare of cultivated land*

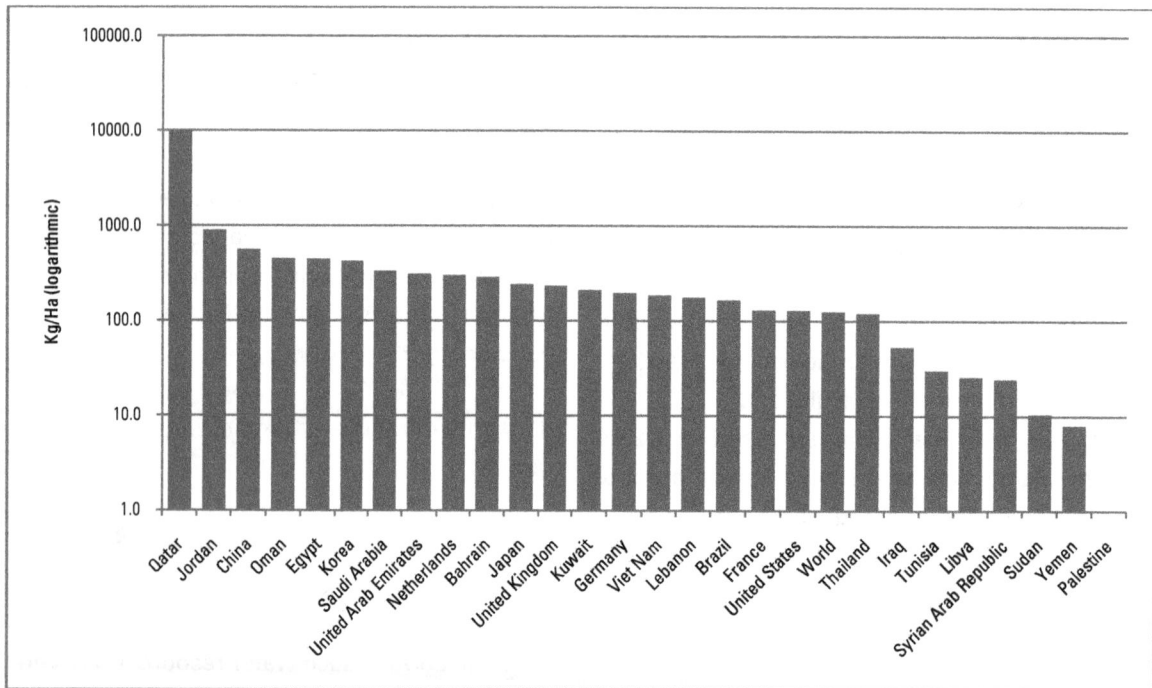

Source: Computed from FAO, FAOSTAT.
Note: Data for Palestine is not available.
   * Cultivated land is defined as arable and permanent crop land.

C. Technology options in the agricultural sector to increase water and energy security

1. Water use efficiency in irrigated agriculture

The water-use-efficiency indicator evaluates the performance of an irrigation system through the ratio of water used against crop production, or actual water requirement and the total amount of water applied. Water-use efficiency for irrigation in the Arab region is estimated at 50 per cent; the proportion of water used for irrigation as compared to the available renewable freshwater resources is close to 60 per cent compared to a global average of less than 10 per cent. The poor level of water-use efficiency in the region is generally attributed to the low opportunity cost of agricultural water, which is artificially maintained through subsidies. Therefore, incentives for farmers and other water users are limited to adopt water-saving technology or to seek ways to use less water per unit of output.[262, 263, 264]

Improved water-use efficiency can be achieved through various means, including appropriate scheduling for water-supply systems, adopting efficient methods of irrigation, wise crop choice and other appropriate agricultural practices. This needs to be accompanied by appropriate policies and the necessary economic and capacity-development tools. Importantly, every unit of water delivered involves energy consumption; therefore, each unit of water unused by the plant involves lost energy, which is consumed while delivering that unit of water to the plant. Thus, improving irrigation efficiency will not only save water but also save energy.[265, 266]

(a) Scheduling water application

The appropriate scheduling of irrigation will minimize water lost through run-off, evaporation or underground percolation, which, in turn, will improve irrigation efficiency and reduce water and energy used. The objective of applying proper appropriate timing and metering irrigation water systems is to maximize profits through the optimization of water and energy usage rather than maximizing yields without due consideration of the amount of water and energy used (box 4).[267, 268]

Box 4. Computer-aided irrigation scheduling in Egypt

In Egypt, attempts have been made to improve irrigation efficiency, namely, through the application of the right amount of water at the right time for maximum yield through an innovative computer-based irrigation scheduling. Maher (2005) assessed the technology's effectiveness and mapped an irrigation schedule that led to substantial savings in water use of more than 100, 128 and 140 million m^3 on corn, groundnut and wheat, respectively. Similarly, Mohammad, al-Ghobari and el-Marazky (2013) reported that the use of an intelligent irrigation scheduling technique led to water savings of more than 20 per cent in the drip irrigation of tomatoes. Several other applications of this technology were successfully used, indicating that the use of computer-aided irrigation scheduling has the potential to lead to substantial savings of water and, related thereto, of energy used to pump that water.

Sources: Maher, 2005; Mohammad, al-Ghobari and el-Marazky, 2013; El-Boraie, Gaber and Abdel-Rahman, 2009; Abdou, and others, 2011.

(b) Irrigation method

Surface irrigation is the most widely used method in the region and is practised on approximately 80 per cent of irrigated areas, followed by sprinkler irrigation at approximately 23 per cent, and microirrigation at only 3 per cent.[269] Although surface or flood irrigation requires less energy, it is the least efficient in terms of water use, which outweighs by far the savings made from lower energy use. Sprinkler irrigation is more water-use efficient than surface irrigation but less so than drip irrigation, which is generally acknowledged to be the most water-efficient irrigation method.

However, as both sprinkler and drip irrigation consume energy through the operation of pumps used to pressurize the water, the initial installation cost of the systems is prohibitive in some cases for poor and smallholder farmers. Box 5 explores the potential water savings achieved through the use of drip irrigation.

> ### Box 5. Irrigation systems in the United Arab Emirates
>
> Sprinkler irrigation is the preferred irrigation method in the United Arab Emirates, despite its inefficiency. However, two new, water-efficient irrigation methods have been introduced. The first method is the well-known drip irrigation, which relies on perforated tubes laid next to the plant on or just beneath the surface. This method drastically decreases evaporation and uses 25 per cent less water compared to a sprinkler system.
>
> The second method is a variant of the drip irrigation system. In this case, pipes are buried some 60 cm below the surface on a water-proof tarp covered by gravel and a corrugated half-pipe to prevent clogging by sand and soil. This method only uses 2.5 litres of water to irrigate a plot that usually requires 10-12 litres.
>
> **Source:** Dakkak, 2015.

> ### Box 6. The buried diffuser irrigation method
>
> Developed by a Tunisian company, the buried diffuser is a localized, underground irrigation technique that can be used in orchards, horticulture and green houses, among others. A porous, mattress-like material buried near the root zone stores water which is gradually released. The method of diffusers, which are linked to the main reservoir and installed in pits or holes at depths of 5-10 cm for crops and 30-70 cm for trees, saves one third of the water utilized in regular drip irrigation, and produces up to four times the output. With less water needed, the diffuser saves up to 70 per cent of energy compared to that of regular drip irrigation systems. Additionally, the diffuser injects water deep into soil layers during the rainy season, which is gradually released during the drier seasons.
>
> **Source:** Chahtech, 2013.
>
> **Note:** The buried diffuser is operational; however, its patent is still pending.

The buried drip system mentioned in box 5 is the most water efficient.[270]However, a buried diffuser developed in Tunisia is claimed to be even more efficient than the buried drip system, however it is more costly (box 6).[271]

(c) Crop choice and other agricultural practices

Increasing water scarcity is an important factor in crop selection. Two factors determine the quantity of water needed: the water demands of particular crops, and the length of their growing period. Rice, sugarcane and bananas have a high water demand compared to citrus fruits, olives or grapes. Similarly, crops with longer growing periods, such as alfalfa or cotton, will require more water than those with much shorter growing periods, including radish, spinach or green beans. For increased water-use efficiency, the proper crop has to be selected depending on the prevailing climatic conditions of the selected area.[272]

Improved agricultural practices also play a major role in water-use efficiency. The use of organic matter and the burying of crop residues have been proven to improve water retention, reducing water run-off and evapotranspiration. With lower water losses, the soil remains moist enough to decrease irrigation. Other practices that might improve water retention or reduce water loss include terracing, ploughing perpendicularly to the slope, which has been practiced for thousands of years in the mountain ranges of Lebanon and Yemen, the use of agroforestry, and improved water distribution infrastructure, all of which offer the potential to improve water use efficiency.[273]

Table 5. Smart agrifood systems: options for water and energy objectives

| Objective | Vulnerability | | | Responses/options |
	Exposure	Sensitivity	Adaptive capacity	
Energy	Increased efficiency	High cost; inadequate practices and technologies	Price variability; increased energy demand and decreased energy efficiency	Decreased dependency on fossil fuels; conservation agriculture; smart irrigation	Energy-efficient technologies; land and crop use change; improved practices (e.g., zero tillage, precision agriculture, crop rotation, low synthetic fertilizers and pesticides); improved logistics
	Increased use of renewable energy in agrifood systems	Lack of capital; low operating knowledge; competition for land and organic matter; increased pressure on water resources; reduced biodiversity	High initial investment cost; potential competition (e.g., land for crops versus biofuels, residues for bioenergy versus animal feed); high price for renewable energy compared to fuel	Decreased dependence on fossil fuels; income diversification; lower climate vulnerability (for wind and solar energy); reduced pollution	On-farm production of renewable energy (solar, wind and biogas)
	Increased access to modern energy services	Higher energy consumption may lead to increased greenhouse gas emissions; may not lead to energy efficiency	Less energy efficiency (e.g., machines using renewable energy might be less efficient)	Energy for production and processing; reduction of food loss; reduced environmental impact; deforestation; greenhouse gas emissions	Provision of modern energy services through renewable forms of energy

Source: Adapted from FAO, 2013a.

Table 6. Smart agrifood systems: options for water and energy ecosystems

Ecosystem		Vulnerability			Responses/options
		Exposure	Sensitivity	Adaptive capacity	
Water	Highlands and rain-fed areas	Rainfall variability; droughts; floods	High: rainfall variability; marginal lands; poor soil moisture capacity	Low: prevalence of poverty; limited options and resources	Watershed management and on-farm water storage for water conservation; integrated water resources management
	River-based irrigation systems	Change in seasonality; reduction of rainfall and runoff; higher occurrence of droughts and floods	High: variations and reduction in water supply as most areas are already under water stress	Low: heavy pressure on water resources; limited possibilities for increased storage and water productivity through conservation measures	Increased water storage and drainage; improved reservoir operations; changes in crop and land use; improved soil and water demand management; revision of drought and flood management plans
	Groundwater-based irrigation systems	Possibilities of increase or decrease of aquifer recharge	High: variations and reduction in water supply as most areas are already under water stress	Low: overexploitation of aquifers and competition with other sectors; limited possibilities in places through increased water productivity	Increased productivity where possible; better groundwater management through controlled pumping; increased water-use efficiency
	Pastoral/grazing lands on fragile soils	High temperatures, rainfall variability, droughts	High: reliance on biomass and water for livestock	Very low: limited options and resources	Better integration of water supply and grazing land management; reduction of livestock density
	Coastal alluvial plains	Sea level rise and salinization of aquifers and estuaries; increased flooding	High:depending on population density and capacity to cope with floods, droughts and salinity levels	Variable	Minimize infrastructure development; better conjunctive use of surface water and groundwater; integrated flood management plans; improved management of coastal aquifers
	Peri-urban agriculture	Depending on location	Relatively low	Highly adaptive and dynamic systems	Focus on competition for water and land with cities, pollution control and health issues

Source: Adapted from FAO, 2013a.

(d) Climate-smart agriculture

Climate-smart agricultural systems provide a new approach to agricultural that addresses food security and climate change. The systems take into account data and information in order to advocate targeted predictive and adaptive decisions that aim to improve sustainability and quality of life and to reduce financial and environmental costs. Given the increasing scarcity of natural resources in the region, a shift in the way land, water and genetic resources are used is a necessity. It requires new thinking in terms of resource management, notably related to governance, policies and financial mechanisms.[274]

Worldwide, the energy sector is responsible for approximately 60 per cent of carbon dioxide emissions, making it the largest contributor to climate change. To this, agrifood systems contribute approximately 20 per cent.[275] Ironically, the impacts of climate change are mostly felt in agrifood systems due to their high demand of water and energy; therefore, climate-smart systems could help enhance the region's capacity to adapt and become resilient to climate change.

Climate-smart agriculture and energy-smart food systems imply managing the region's water resources more efficiently while promoting a low carbon food economy, notably through the adoption of practices and technologies that sustainably improve yields and productivity, support adaptation to extreme events, including droughts and floods, but also higher costs of energy, while also reducing levels of greenhouse gases. Income diversification that allows stakeholders to obtain alternative means to survive and adopt climate- and energy-smart systems is part of a smart-system economy. Tables 5 and 6 review selected options for improved water and energy-use efficiency, which form the basis of a smart agrifood system.

2. Treated wastewater reuse

Several countries in the Arab region have resorted to non-conventional water resources practices, mainly desalination and treated wastewater, in order to bridge the gap between conventional water resources supply and water demand. Reusing treated wastewater is less energy-intensive than desalinating but energy intensity varies with the size of the treatment plant, requirement of regulations on treated effluent water quality and the technology utilized. The energy demands for various treatment processes of a large wastewater treatment facility are approximately 0.22 kWh/m^3 for a trickling filter, 0.27 kwh/m^3 for activated sludge, 0.31 kWh/m^3 for advanced treatment, and 0.41 kWh/m^3 for advanced treatment with nitrification.[276] However, these values are indicative only and vary with regions and climate conditions.

The energy demand of treated wastewater may be offset by strict energy efficiency measures during the design and operation of such facilities and by the selection of appropriate technologies to match local climate conditions. This is seen in anaerobic digestion, which is an energy-efficient process well suited to the warm climate of the Arab region and allows for the production of biogas. Recovered biogas may be used for onsite generation of heat and electricity and even for offsite energy production. Anaerobic processes can also be more energy-efficient in the sense that they require less energy for aeration to maintain the dissolved oxygen levels for aerobic bacterial growth. An example of this can be found at the As-Samra Waste Water Treatment Plant, the largest wastewater treatment plant in Jordan that serves a population of 2.27 million with a dry weather flow of 267,000 m^3/day. Hydraulic potential energy at the inlet and outlet of the plant produces 3.35MW of electricity, which is further augmented by 5.375 MW through a biogas-powered generator created from an anaerobic sludge digester,[277] to achieve 80 per cent self-sufficiency.[278]

Treated wastewater in the Arab region is mainly used for irrigation and industrial cooling systems. In general, treated wastewater can be used for the irrigation of crop, green spaces and golf courses, as is already practiced to a high degree in the Gulf region, for industrial cooling and, more recently, for groundwater aquifer recharge. Two conditions govern the use of wastewater, which are the level of treatment, namely, whether primary, secondary or tertiary level, and the location of the treatment plant in relation to the end users.

The main setback of wastewater reuse in many Arab countries has been the lack of adoption and enforcement of wastewater treatment standards specific to each end use, for instance crop irrigation. Although several countries, including Jordan, Kuwait, Oman, Saudi Arabia, Tunisia and Yemen, have produced their own standards for wastewater reuse, other such countries as Bahrain have adopted WHO and FAO standards while again other countries, such as Egypt, Iraq and Lebanon, have no specific standards for wastewater reuse.[279] The increase in urbanization makes the reuse of wastewater ideal for peri-urban agriculture location a suitable solution, especially keeping in mind that generated wastewater increases proportionally to increased population.

The volume of treated municipal wastewater for direct use is over 2.9km³/year for 16 out of 22 Arab countries.[280] This significant value nearly equals the reported volume of produced desalinated water of 3.2km³/year for 18 out of 22 Arab countries.[281] Therefore, treated wastewater is increasingly becoming a main component of national water resources management plans in the Arab region.

Jordan is one of the leading countries in the region to utilize treated wastewater. There are several factors central to the country adopting an aggressive wastewater-reuse strategy. Most significant is its per capita share of renewable water resources of 128.8 m³/capita/year as of 2014.[282] Since the early 1980s, the Government of Jordan has implemented considerable plans in the wastewater sector. This has resulted in a significant increase in the volume of wastewater collected from most cities and towns, which is currently being treated in 21treatment plants at a volume of nearly 120 MCM annually.[283, 284]

The early establishment of national standards for treated effluents has greatly helped in the acceptance of its use, although strict quality enforcement is an ongoing requirement. The treated wastewater is mainly used by the agriculture sector for irrigation in the Jordan valley and to a lesser extent by the industry. Treated wastewater is also part of Jordan's national water strategy and currently accounts for nearly 15 per cent of available resources (figure 12). This allows for the re-allocation of the freshwater resources that would have been used in the agriculture sector to the domestic sector without greatly impacting the available irrigation water.

Figure 12. Current and projected treated wastewater usage as per Jordan's National Water Strategy, 2008-2022

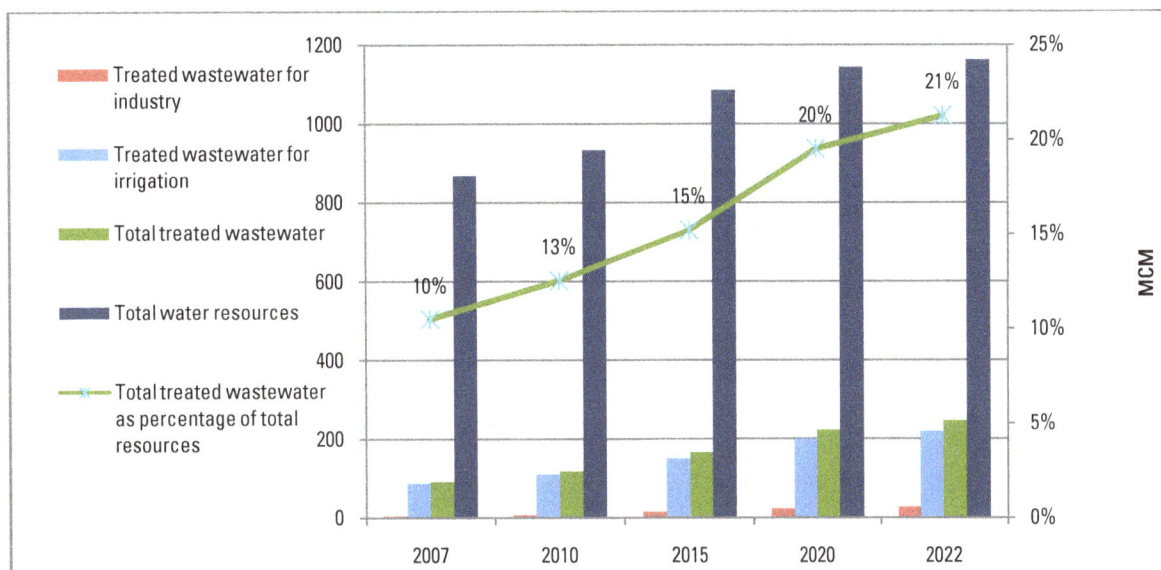

Source: Adapted from Ministry of Water and Irrigation, 2009.
Note: Total resources for the year 2022 are without the Red-Dead Sea conveyance project.

D. Investing abroad for increased food security

1. Foreign investments as a means for water-scarce Arab countries to ensure food security

Due to the increasing scarcity of natural resources and high population growth, several countries from the region are opting to invest in the acquisition of farmland in various parts of the world in the hope of producing determined proportions of food offshore. Arab countries are not alone in investing in farmland overseas. However, while Arab countries do so in an attempt to cover their food and feed gap deficits, most other countries carry out such investments as part of a strategy to diversify investments and tap into promising new markets.

Such investments are being made in Africa, Latin America, South-East Asia and increasingly in Eastern Europe. Most deals, which range from investments of 10,000 ha or less to hundreds of thousands of hectares, are mainly made by private investors and only a few by Governments. International deals are usually made by large corporations and global financial institutions.[285, 286]

The impact of land deals is still dubious in most cases; however, for the countries in which investments are being made, they are credited with enhancing technology acquisition and innovation, improving infrastructure, generating on- and off-farm employment, and increasing food production. However, in the case of developing countries, this practice often raises concerns about land grabbing as some of the deals lead to the displacement of local farmers, the unsustainable use of land and water resources, increasing local food insecurity and impediments to the rights of the local population. For investing countries aiming to secure access to food, tangible evidence has yet to be provided that the objective of food security is being met in all or at least in part as the countries involved in these foreign land investments continue to acquire the food they need through regular international channels.

However, land acquisitions are unlikely to stop due to the continuing economic growth in emerging countries that are also some of the world's most populous countries, including Brazil, China, India and Indonesia, which require increasing amounts of food. Countries in the region are expected to continue this practice as well due to the growing scarcity of natural resources, the fear of increased competition and the possible disruption in global food markets; and land deals offer preferential trading options.

2. Investments

Available data on foreign land investment indicates that deals concerning Arab countries involved approximately 2.6 million ha of land, with options of expansion to cover approximately 5.7 million ha.[287] However, so far only approximately 65,000 ha are actually being exploited. Arab countries receiving investments include Egypt, Mauritania, Morocco, the Sudan, and Tunisia, as detailed in table 7.

Table 7. Foreign land investment involving Arab countries

Country	Size of contract (ha)	Option to increase size (ha)	Actual exploitation (ha)
Arab countries receiving investments			
Egypt	68,000	134,000	10,000
Mauritania	5,000	5,000	0
Morocco	701,000	702,000	800
Sudan	529,000	1,297,000	15,000
Tunisia	4,000	0	0
Largest Arab investors abroad			
Saudi Arabia	1,493,000	1,450,000	41,200
United Arab Emirates	437,000	2,836,000	5,600
Largest Arab investments in non-Arab countries			
Ethiopia	546,000	308,000	6,000
South Sudan	105,000	2,490,000	300

Source: Land Matrix, n.d.

Investing Arab countries include Bahrain, Djibouti, Egypt, Kuwait, Lebanon, Libya, Qatar, Saudi Arabia, the Sudan, Syrian Arab Republic and United Arab Emirates, with the largest deals being made by Saudi Arabia and the United Arab Emirates. Arab countries invested in non-Arab countries, including Argentina, Benin, the Democratic Republic of Congo, Ethiopia, Ghana, India, Malaysia, Malawi, Mali, Mozambique, Pakistan, Philippines, Senegal, Sierra Leone, South Africa, South Sudan, Tanzania, Turkey, and Ukraine, with the majority of the deals carried out in Ethiopia and South Sudan. The largest single deal by an Arab country has been concluded with the Ukraine, with Saudi Arabia exploiting approximately 29,000 ha to produce wheat. Non-Arab countries investing in Arab countries include Brazil, China, India, Japan, Korea, and Spain.

Additionally, there are land deals of approximately 6.6 million ha that are currently being negotiated by Arab countries, with the bulk being in Indonesia (2.1 million ha), the Sudan (2.1 million ha), Uganda (840,000 ha), Philippines (428,000 ha), Pakistan (364,000 ha), and Cote d'Ivoire (300,000 ha). Furthermore, it is worth noting that negotiations on land deals have failed or contracts have been cancelled for unstated reasons with an area of 1.5 million ha in question. Table 7 shows that the actual amount of exploited land tends to be considerably less than the area covered by land contracts or the area which is actually available for cultivation.

The largest number of land deals was made by private investors, including MIDROC Group, Al Qudra Holding, Al Rajhi Group, Hassad Food, Qalaa Holdings, and Noor. These were followed by deals made by financial groups, including the National Bank of Egypt, Foras International Investment Company, Pharos Financial Group, and Renaissance Capital, and a few deals made by Government institutions, including the Abu Dhabi Fund for Development, Sudan National Pension Fund, Kuwait Investment Authority, Public Investment Fund of Saudi Arabia, and RAK Investment Authority, just to name a few.

As Woertz (2011)[288] notes, there seems to be more hype surrounding these land deals than truth. Except for Saudi Arabia's land investment in the Ukraine, most deals involved local actors who led the operations on the ground. MIDROC Ethiopia, for instance, is owned by a Saudi-Ethiopian who has many more investments in Ethiopia.

Most countries targeted by land investments are not well known for their food exort capacity and face major food security and concerns over water availability. Thus, it is highly unlikely that they would allow the export of locally produced food without first meeting national demands. Infrastructure with foreign agricultural investment inflows to support production, transport and export of food on a large scale or in a cost-effective manner in these countries is limited. Therefore, in order to benefit from land investments, tied assistance in the development of local capacities and infrastructure is needed.

3. Interregional and intraregional trade

The Arab region is unable to produce the food it requires relying solely on water and land resources available at the national and regional levels. Given that water scarcity is expected to worsen in the advent of climate change, the region will increasingly have to fulfil its food need through trade. This can mean the import of water and virtual water trade, a concept that refers to the water embedded in the production of agricultural products, which could allow water-poor countries to meet some of their water requirements through trade.

Table 8. Total renewable water resources and net virtual water import per capita per year in selected Arab countries

Country	Total renewable water resources (m³/capita) 1993-1997	Total renewable water resources (m³/capita) 2014	Net virtual water import: crop and livestock (m³/capita) 1995-1999
Algeria	385	298	350
Bahrain	194	87	641
Comoros	2499	1633	157
Djibouti	436	343	189
Egypt	924	710	255
Iraq	4142	2661	72
Jordan	206	129	957
Kuwait	12	6	682
Lebanon	1456	934	446
Libya	142	113	259
Mauritania	4604	2931	151
Morocco	1050	879	203
Oman	643	386	650
Qatar	110	25	540
Saudi Arabia	126	83	625
Somalia	2203	1401	33
Sudan	5043	996	-51
Syrian Arab Republic	1108	767	-264
Tunisia	500	420	424
United Arab Emirates	58	16	1396
Yemen	131	86	92

Sources: FAO, 2013b; World Bank, n.d.b; Hoekstra, 2003.

Efforts have been made to quantify virtual water trade flows, which have been shown to exceed 1,000 billion m^3 worldwide. Approximately 13 per cent of the water is used to produce the 38 primary crops worldwide, which are consumed in a country other than the producing one.[289] As one of the world's major wheat and cereal net importers, the Arab region, and especially GCC countries, stands to greatly benefit from virtual water trade.[290] In the Arab region, the net virtual water import per capita through crop and livestock represents a sizable portion when compared to the region's total renewable water resources, with only the Sudan and the Syrian Arab Republic as net exporters (table 8).

Therefore, virtual water trade should be seen as a relevant water-harnessing strategy given the prevailing water scarcity in the region. Importantly, the region needs to acknowledge that by exporting locally produced agricultural products, it is in fact also exporting its scarce water.[291] Furthermore, it should be noted that the energy component embedded in the food is also part of this trade, which is brought to the forefront in the WEF security nexus.

V. Conclusions and Recommendations

The current state of the water, energy and food sectors in the Arab region strongly suggests the need for a shift in the current segmented and uncoordinated sectoral management of the natural resources to a more integrated natural resources management approach that reduces waste, increases efficiency, considers the implications of climate change, and leads to more sustainable development for the region. However, if the WEF nexus is pursued from a people-centred approach, it is preferable to frame the interdependencies between these sectors from the perspective of a WEF security nexus approach that is based on the right to development and ensuring water, energy and food for all. A new holistic systems approach is thus needed to pursue the management of the natural resources and the delivery of basic services that breaks the silo mentality and generates win-win opportunities focusing on synergies rather than conflicts and competition across sectors.

The unbalanced distribution of natural resources endowments across the region is among the reasons why a WEF security nexus approach can help to decompose the complex relationships that characterize WEF security. The pressures on the region's natural resources are many and have multisectoral implications that include increasing population and improved standards of living, which increase demands on water and energy resources and services. More food is sourced from more protein and wheat-based diets that require water for cultivation and livestock rearing, and the energy to process, store and deliver the food to market. In many Arab countries, this vicious cycle is poorly managed by the isolated sectoral mainstream approach. The distributional dimensions of securing water, energy and food for all from a human rights-based perceptive or a gender perspective further complicate the cycle. The challenges resulting therefrom are momentous even without considering the implications of their changing production and consumption patterns on ecosystems degradation in face of climate change.

The WEF security nexus analytical framework provides an original paradigm for integrated natural resources management. Although not a new concept, the WEF nexus is best suited to a cross-sectoral approach, while other such approaches as IWRM and sustainable rural livelihood are centred on one sector or interest group with other sectors more or less servicing that sector. The WEF security nexus presents an analytical framework that may be shaped by users to match various interests, scales, and internal and external stress factors. This flexibility, together with the ability of users to modify the nexus analytical framework to be all-inclusive yet matching the actual scale and scenario is its main advantage.

The report has explored simple to complex approaches to the nexus that include several pillars of importance. It is advisable to start with a simple yet robust nexus analytical framework, increasing its complexity as further elements become available. Furthermore, the WEF security nexus analytical framework approach is well suited for the Arab region. Some of the challenges presented by the shared water resources in the Arab region have been briefly examined in view of the suitability of a WEF security nexus management approach that aids in conflict resolution and promotes cooperation across transboundary shared water resources. In addition, the interdependencies between water, energy and food are explored in the light of achieving sustainable development and improved security in the region through increased efficiency, resource optimization and technological innovations, among others. The success of such a nexus approach hinges in part on institutional mechanisms ready to address the challenges of the region through appropriate strategies, plans and policies stemming from a human rights-based perspective at a scale best suited for the case at hand. The following are key conclusions and recommendations of the report.

A. Implications of the nexus for integrated natural resources management

The recent series of global and regional events, including economic crises, climate variability and armed conflicts accentuates the need to revaluate the region's approach to natural resources planning and management. The current silo mentality across the region has been unsuccessful in addressing the fall-out from these events, even though the natural resources in many parts of the region have reached dangerous thresholds and have even crossed them in other parts where the equilibrium of natural states has been breached.

Given its holistic approach, the WEF security nexus is well suited for integrated natural resources planning and management. This can be best achieved and maintained through well-established institutional mechanisms at the national and regional levels in order to enable the WEF security nexus and support integrated planning and coherent policymaking.

At the national level, many Arab countries have the skeletal framework in place, with many of the ministries having under their mandate two or more such sectors as water and electricity, water and energy or water and agriculture. In a number of countries, this nucleus needs to be strengthened through the empowerment of cross-sectoral integrated planning under the joint mandate of those ministries which had previously dealt with these issues individually. It is more efficient to take advantage of existing ministries and other institutions in order to enact the nexus approach that engages stakeholders and builds capacities at al levels, while respecting good governance practices. This institutional nexus mechanism approach would aim at achieving coherence across policies and initiatives through the identification of synergies and win-win situations.

At the regional level, the WEF security nexus offers possible opportunities for conflict resolution, especially where resources are shared between two or more countries. Again, in order for the nexus to become operational and be beneficial, regional institutional mechanisms are needed to address the diverse challenges facing the region. In this regard, ESCWA inter-governmental committees and League of Arab States intergovernmental councils are already facilitating cooperation and work on the WEF security nexus at the regional level.

ESCWA has been active in examining the nexus over the last several years and convened two intergovernmental consultative meetings on the water and energy nexus in the Arab region. A set of priorities and initiatives were identified by the water resources and energy committees for future work. Based on these priorities, ESCWA launched various activities, including two projects for regional capacity development on the WEF security nexus. The first project addresses capacity development of ESCWA member countries in the water-energy nexus in order to achieve SDGs, which through various means will develop and disseminate a set of seven regional policy toolkits and three technical toolkits. The second project deals with the promotion of food and water security through cooperation and capacity development in the Arab region. This project specifically aims at strengthening the capacity to assess impacts of changing water availability on agricultural production in the Arab region, enhancing the capacity of interregional coordinated policy development for food and water security, and improving the capacity to assess the status of food security and the efficiency of food production.

In addition to the above, the League of Arab States is pursuing activities on the WEF nexus through the Arab Ministerial Council on Electricity and the Arab Ministerial Water Council and with the support of GIZ and ESCWA. GIZ is also collaborating with the Arabian Gulf University to produce policy briefs on the WEF nexus, which aim to foster regional dialogue on the nexus.

There are other semi-regional institutions, including NBI and OSS, that are not dedicated to or do not officially work under a nexus mandate. However, they are positioned to perform integrated water recourses management in a shared basin setting, such as the NBI and the OSS. In a shared basin, the WEF security nexus can help to build cooperation through natural intersectoral synergies where single-sector approaches have failed in the past to bridge the mutual benefit gap.

Academic and scientific research centres or think tanks can play a very important role in support of the nexus through innovative applied research, increasing the knowledge base on nexus interactions, and spearheading national and regional nexus dialogue. However, there are very few, if any, nexus-dedicated centres or curricula to combine the concerns of the three sectors under one umbrella. These centres are usually the birthplace of much needed local technological innovations to advance cross-sectoral efficiency gains, which are key to achieving nexus synergies.

With a view to minimizing negative trade-offs across sectors at the regional level, it is imperative that the nexus approach ensures coherence across strategies, plans, policies, and initiatives, taking into account differing regional natural resource endowments. Fragmented strategies and policies weaken the overall resilience of the region and result in competition over limited resources, including weakened adaptability to such externalities as climate change. The effects of climate change, for instance, do not hit a particular sector and country, but much rather resonate across a wide spectrum. If properly institutionalized, the WEF security nexus approach has the potential to effectively harmonize these interactions across sectors and countries.

B. Insights for informing the Sustainable Development Goals

1. A people-centred human rights-based approach to water, energy and food security

The Rio+20 United Nations Conference on Sustainable Development outcome document, The Future We Want, signaled the international community's strong will to continue to pursue sustainable development, with more comprehensive SDGs replacing the MDGs. The new SDGs seem to better acknowledge sustainable development interlinkages among various environmental, social and economic dimensions of development. The WEF security nexus analytical framework with its holistic systems approach can assist along this path, providing the necessary foundation for informing decision makers of potential synergies and win-win situations for achieving sustainable development from a people-centred approach, based on the universal human rights principle that can provide a common denominator for dialogue and decision-making across ministries and countries. SDGs 2, 6 and 7 are of particular relevance to the WEF security nexus in the Post-2015 Development Agenda, which relate to ensuring access to food, water and sustainable energy for all.

The WEF security nexus analytical framework can be used to provide insight on the coherence of achieving these goals, optimizing possible synergies and avoiding unintentional negative feedback. It can also aid in avoiding pitfalls in the holistic analysis of all sectors in order to inform policymakers on potential system synergies and conflicts at all levels from policy formulation to implementation.

The wording of the SDGs has been carefully selected to reflect the principles of human rights in terms of availability, accessibility, affordability, and sustainability across generations. This perspective considers the access to water, energy and food as a human right necessary for sustainable development and not as a commodity that may be controlled by individuals, corporations or States either through ownership, location or boundaries.

This is perhaps the most suitable approach for the WEF security nexus in the Arab region, given the varying natural resource endowments, the existing economic disparity within and between nations and social unrest and armed conflict. However, this approach does not negate the economic value of these resources but calls for balancing their economic value with the understanding that they are considered human rights in terms of accessibility, affordability, reliability, and sustainability. For instance, the use of targeted and innovative subsidies in the agriculture sector that encourage efficiency and improved practices instead of the common blanket subsidies that seem to benefit mostly large farming corporations but lack a drive for improvement, leading to low sector efficiency and increasing amounts of waste across all sectors in many countries of the region.

Social unrest, armed conflicts and occupation render the pursuit of change in the region currently very difficult. A diligent nexus analysis that is participatory and engages stakeholders at all levels can help to identify win-win situations and support implementation on the ground. The current natural resources approach has failed to secure urban and rural equality in water, energy and food security. In terms of access to resources and the reliability of services, urban centres as places of political and economic power are generally much better off than rural and even peri-urban localities. This leads to a vicious cycle of urban growth and economic development at the expense of ecosystem degradation, economic disparity and unsustainable development. Therefore, this is the ideal entry point for the WEF security nexus with a human focus that provides overarching analysis balancing economic and social interactions across sectors.

Following the lines of a human rights-based approach, SE4All was used to guide the development of the energy-related SDG with three main objectives, namely, to ensure universal access to modern energy services; double the global rate of improvement of energy efficiency; and double the share of renewable energy in the global energy mix. These objectives have potentially significant spillover effects into other sectors.

Improved universal access to modern energy services has the potential to enhance the delivery and reliability of water services. More energy for the agriculture sector can improve access to water supply, especially for areas dependent on groundwater, and can serve to reduce post-harvest losses. Improved energy

efficiency can reduce the amount of water used by the energy sector, thereby availing more water to other sectors. Finally, doubling the share of renewable energy will provide new sustainable means of energy supply.

These objectives have a significant role to play in the three sectors and can be entirely captured only through the WEF nexus analytical framework. A regional agenda has been proposed for the implementation of the SE4All goals including required policy reforms, technological innovations, finance and investment, and analysis and monitoring following its launch in the region by the representative of the United Nations Secretary-General and ESCWA in Amman in March 2015.

2. The water-energy-food security nexus scale of analysis

An all-inclusive and participatory approach that engages stakeholders across sectors at all levels will greatly aid in identifying the appropriate scale of analysis. However, the variations in resource endowments across the Arab region require the WEF security nexus analytical framework to be practical, adaptive and flexible. It should be utilized at the appropriate scale where strategies and policies stand to benefit from national to regional scale analysis while plans and projects, in general, are better dealt with at the local to national scale. However, regarding projects dealing with shared resources, the framework is better matched to the basin level and may play a constructive role in conflict resolution and improved cooperation.

Similarly, the WEF security nexus analysis scale should consider external stresses, including, among others, climate change, population growth, and ecosystem degradation.

3. Efficiency and resource optimization through nexus-related technology choices

The natural resources available in the region are unable to meet the current demand, especially when the projected growth rate is considered. Improved efficiency across sectors is crucial for waste reduction and resource optimization in order to achieve more with less through technological innovations guided by the WEF security nexus. For example, improved technological efficiencies in the water sector through the utilization of efficient pumps will lead to energy savings, more efficient energy technologies will reduce the water intensity of power generation and technologically modernized agriculture will reduce stress on the water resources and improve productivity. Efficiency and resource optimization have to be coupled with local innovation supported through local to regional research and development. Local technological innovations coupled with accelerated access are another opportunity for income generation and economic development for the poor.

Technological choices must be related to the nexus at an appropriate scale where an increase in water security is translated into an increase in energy and food security. Technology choices may also need appropriate policies to accelerate access and maximize benefits across sectors. Efficiency focused on one sector may lead to negative impacts in other sectors if not properly related through the nexus.

C. Recommendations

The WEF security nexus presents a genuine opportunity for the region to move towards integrated natural resources management. In the last few years, there has been growing momentum surrounding the nexus that the Arab region has partly joined. However, a nexus approach should be actively tailored to the region's natural resources endowments, specificities, challenges, and strengths in order to support sustainable development and improve water, energy and food security within a human rights-based framework. There is a need to engage a wide range of stakeholders from all sectors concerned to facilitate a multilevel and interdisciplinary dialogue. Regional expert group meetings such as the two already organized by ESCWA can facilitate dialogue and should be complemented with meetings at the national level.

In the short to medium term, the establishment of a regional nexus knowledge hub would address cross-sectoral datasets essential for nexus analysis. Datasets would help to understand the linkages between the three sectors and the social implications across the region's demographics. With support through Government funding and improved access to capital through loan guarantees, the knowledge hub should be complemented with a clear policy to support regional and local innovation, and applied research and development with the objectives to improve cross-sectoral efficiency gains and reduce wastage.

The nexus is a dynamic process that requires appropriate feedback mechanisms. Consultations should be held to identify local and regional indicators in order to facilitate monitoring, assessment and knowledge sharing, which could also be shared in the nexus knowledge hub.

Institutionalizing the nexus is a priority in order for it to be operationalized. At the regional level, ESCWA and the League of Arab States can play an important role in the coordination and provision of the technical assistance needed for applying the nexus. At the national level, several countries in the region have the basis for nexus ministries with two or more sectors under their mandate. Where such ministries exist, a true nexus approach through policy and mandate reforms should be activated. Similarly, a few shared water resources basins have coordination committees in place, which must be steered to cooperate and manage within a nexus framework. Thus, the priority is to reform and empower existing nexus management bodies; where no such organs exist, however, mechanisms should be established enabling core line ministries of water, energy and agriculture to work closely together for the sake of policy integration and harmonization.

The region's chronic and critical shortage of natural water resources coupled with the agricultural sector being the largest water consumer makes water the highest priority. Technological innovations are urgently needed to improve water-use efficiency while increasing agriculture productivity. Furthermore, national and regional research and development must focus on ways how to improve both water and food security through energy savings and conservation. A considerable amount of the region's water resources could be shifted from supplying agricultural demands to supplying other such sectors as domestic use. These objectives require associated policies regarding water management and agriculture. In broad terms, there is consensus on the technical solutions to address the objectives of national plans for water resources such as new, efficient irrigation techniques and reallocation of water shares. However, financing and institutional implementation of these measures in a sustainable way present major challenges and call for a paradigm shift in management and subsidy policies. Food imports also play an important role in improving food security and in providing water savings through the virtual water trade; however, this has to be balanced with the risks of price volatility, local social and economic impacts and political stability.

Treated wastewater reuse is a significant resource that many countries are failing to fully utilize. Clear quality guidelines and control mechanisms are needed to encourage treated wastewater reuse for various users resulting in water savings and even energy savings. Additionally, renewable energy use and improved efficiency for desalination and at all stages of the water sector should be promoted given the significant water-energy interlinkages and potential for savings. Reducing the amount of water that is unaccounted for has the multiple benefits of saving water and the energy required to deliver this water.

The region's great potential for improving energy security through improved efficiency and renewable sources should be further supported, keeping in focus the different energy endowments across the region and the available water and land resources needed for various energy sources. Energy trade has an important role to play in the WEF security nexus, but it necessitates the development of regional transmission grids for regional trade and the improvement of national grids for local energy exchange.

Furthermore, the nexus approach for medium to long-term analysis must draw upon climate change assessments, specifically those assessments developed for the Arab region such as the Regional Initiative for the Assessment the Impact of Climate Change on Water Resources and Socio-Economic Vulnerability in the Arab Region. The impacts of climate change must be accounted for in nexus-related analysis and decision-making. A final entry point is demand-side management and behavioural change. These should target the domestic, industrial and agricultural sector through specific media and tools in order to modify consumption patterns at the medium to long-term scale, resulting in savings in water and energy across the WEF nexus.

By combining these three components with a view to the dynamics caused by climate change and the need to ensure access to basic human rights associated with the right to food, water, sanitation, development, and energy, the WEF security nexus can provide an effective analytical framework that can assist Arab States in achieving progress towards sustainable development.

Bibliography

Moubidine, Issam (2013). Minister of Interior requests Southern companies to evacuate farms and buildings immediately. Assabeel, November 4. Available from http://www.assabeel.net/local/item/11785 (in Arabic).

Abdel Gelil, Ibrahim, and others, eds. (2013). *2013 Report of the Arab Forum for Environment and Development (AFED), Arab Environment 6: Sustainable Energy - Prospects, Challenges, Opportunities.* Beirut: AFED. Available from http://www.afedonline.org/Report2013/english.html.

Abdou, S.M.M., and others (2011). Response of Sunflower Yield and Water Relations to Sowing Dates and Irrigation Scheduling Under Middle Egypt Conditions. *Advances in Applied Science Research*, vol. 2, No. 3, pp. 141-150. Available from http://pelagiaresearchlibrary.com/advances-in-applied-science/vol2-iss3/AASR-2011-2-3-141-150.pdf.

Abu-Zeid, Khaled (2008). Water in the Mediterranean: Green Water and Effective Legislation for Transboundary Water Management. European Institute of the Mediterranean. Available from http://www.iemed.org/anuari/2008/aarticles/EN89.pdf.

Al-Ahmadi, Masoud E. (2009). Hydrogeology of the Saq Aquifer Northwest of Tabuk, Northern Saudi Arabia. *Journal of King Abdulaziz University-Earth Sciences,* vol. 20, No. 1, pp. 51-66. 13 May. Available from http://www.kau.edu.sa/Files/195/Researches/58775_29052.pdf.

Al Lawati, Y. (2014). Oil Produced Water is a Promising Unconventional Source of Water. Presentation on Use of Unconventional Water in Urban Water Management.

Al-Zubari, Waleed (2014). The Costs of Municipal Water Supply in Bahrain. *Valuing Vital Resources in the Gulf Series.* London: Chatham House (December). Available from http://www.chathamhouse.org/sites/files/chathamhouse/field/field_document/20141216Municipal WaterBahrainAlZubari.pdf.

Andrews-Speed, Philip, and others (2012). *The Global Resource Nexus: The Struggles for Land, Energy, Food, Water, and Minerals.* Washington, D.C.: Transatlantic Academy. Available from http://www.bosch-stiftung.de/content/language2/downloads/TA_2012_report_web_version.pdf.

Arab Group for the Protection of Nature (n.d.). Arab Network for Food Sovereignty. Available from http://apnature.org/en/content/arab-network-food-sovereignty.

Arab Ministerial Council of Electricity (2015). Report of Arab Ministerial Council of Electricity meeting, Cairo, 9 June 2015. Egypt (in Arabic).

Arab Union of Electricity (2013). Statistical Bulletin for 2013. Issue 22. Available from http://www.auptde.org/Article_Files/2013.pdf (in Arabic).

Attar, Abdelmajid (n.d.). L'ancien *DG De Sonatrach Abdelmadjid Attar: le Gouvernement Doit Reviser Ses Investissements*. YouTube. Available from http://www.youtube.com/watch?v=57wcdmKty6E. Accessed in April 2015.

Awulachew, Seleshi B., and others, eds. (2012). *The Nile River Basin: Water, Agriculture, Governance and Livelihoods*. International Water Management Institute. New York: Routledge.

Badr, Karine (2010). Rural women and agriculture in the MENA. Centre International de Hautes Etudes Agronomiques Mediterraneennes (CIHEAM) Briefing Notes No. 66 (May). Paris.

Barrouhi, Abdelaziz (2008). L'art et la manière de gérer l'eau. *Jeune Afrique*, 19 May. Available from http://www.jeuneafrique.com/Article/LIN18058larteuaelre0/ (in French).

Barthelemy, Y., and others (2007). Modelling of the Saq aquifer system (Saudi Arabia). In *Aquifer system management: Darcy's legacy in a world of impending water shortage*. IAH, Dijon Symposium, Dijon, France.

Becker, Markus (2012). Contaminated Aquifers: Radioactive Water Threatens Middle East. *Spiegel Online International*. 5 November. Available from http://www.spiegel.de/international/world/contaminated-aquifers-radioactive-water-threatens-middle-east-a-865290.html.

Beckman, Jayson, Allison Borchers and Carol A. Jones (2013). Agriculture's supply and demand for energy and energy products. *Economic Information Bulletin*, No. 112. Washington, D.C.: Economic Research Service, United States Department of Agriculture (May). Available from http://www.ers.usda.gov/media/1104145/eib112.pdf.

Besbes, Mustapha, and others (2002). Conceptual framework of the North Western Sahara Aquifer System. Proceedings of the International workshop of managing shared aquifer resources in Africa, Tripoli, Libya, 2-4 June. Available from http://www.isarm.org/dynamics/modules/SFIL0100/view.php?fil_Id=192.

Bizikova, Livia, and others (2013). The Water-Energy-Food Security Nexus: Towards a practical planning and decision-support framework for landscape investment and risk management. IISD Report. Winnipeg: International Institute for Sustainable Development (IISD) (February). Available from http://www.iisd.org/pdf/2013/wef_nexus_2013.pdf.

Boelee, Eline, Eric Hoa and Thomas Chiramba (2014). UNEP's engagement in the water-energy-food nexus. Prepared in connection with the Conference on Sustainability in the Water-Energy-Food Nexus, Bonn, 19 May. Available from http://wef-conference.gwsp.org/uploads/media/B03_Boelee.pdf.

Bradbrook, Adrian J., and Judith G. Gardam (2006). Placing Access to Energy Services within a Human Rights Framework. *Human Rights Quarterly*, vol. 28, pp. 389-415. Available from http://muse.jhu.edu/login?auth=0&type=summary&url=/journals/human_rights_quarterly/v028/28.2bradbrook.pdf.

Bryden, John, Lily Riahi and Romain Zissler (2013). *MENA Renewables Status Report*. Paris: REN21 Secretariat.

Busche, Daniel, and Bassam Hayek (2015). Energy efficiency in water pumping in Jordan. Presented during the meeting on Energy Efficiency in the MENA Region: Good Practices from ACWUA Member Utilities, Third Arab Water Week, Amman, January. Available from http://arabwaterweek.com/UploadFile/Presentation/261201551195En2-Daniel%20Busche%20and%20Bassam%20Hayek.pdf.

Center for Sustainable Systems, University of Michigan (2014). Unconventional Fossil Fuels Factsheet. Pub. No. CSS13-19. Available from http://css.snre.umich.edu/css_doc/CSS13-19.pdf.

Chahtech (2013). The Buried Diffuser: A real innovation for an efficient irrigation. Chahbani Technologies (June). Available from http://www.chahtech.com/doc/en/Buried-Diffuser-English-Report.pdf.

Chouchane, Hatem, and others (2014). The water footprint of Tunisia from an economic perspective. *Ecological Indicators*, vol. 52, pp. 311-319. Available from http://www.waterfootprint.org/Reports/Chouchane-et-al-2015.pdf.

Christian, L. (2000). Middle East Geological Map Series (MEG-Maps). Manama: Gulf PetroLink.

Committee on Economic, Social and Cultural Rights (1999). The Right to Adequate Food (Art. 11). Contained in Document E/C.12/1999/5 (12 May).

Cour des comptes (2014). Le cout de production de l'électricité nucléaire: actualisation 2014. Communication a la Commission d'Enquete de l'Asseblee Nationale (May). Available from https://www.ccomptes.fr/content/download/68537/1858246/version/2/file/20140527_rapport_cout_production_electricite_nucleaire.pdf.

Dabour, Nabil (2006). Water resources and their use in agriculture in Arab countries. *Journal of Economic Cooperation*, vol. 27, No. 1, pp. 1-38. Available from http://www.sesrtcic.org/files/article/25.pdf.

Dakkak, Amir (2015). Irrigation systems in the United Arab Emirates. *EcoMENA*, 31 January. Available from http://www.ecomena.org/irrigation-systems-in-uae/.

Darem, Faisal (2015). Yemen encourages farmers to use solar energy in irrigation. *Al-Shorfa.com*, 9 January. Available from http://al-shorfa.com/en_GB/articles/meii/features/2015/01/09/feature-03. Accessed in May 2015.

Darwish, M. A., N. M. al-Najem and N. Lior (2009). Towards sustainable seawater desalting in the Gulf area. *Desalination*, vol. 235, pp. 58-87. Available from http://www.seas.upenn.edu/~lior/lior%20papers/Towards%20sustainable%20seawater%20desalting%20in%20the%20Gulf%20area%20-published.pdf.

Degremont Jordan (2008). Samra Wastewater Treatment Plant Jordan. Available from http://www.degremont.com/document/?f=engagements/en/samra-wastewater-treatment-plant.pdf.

Economic and Social Commission for Western Asia (ESCWA) (2009a). *Knowledge Management and Analysis of ESCWA Member Countries Capacities in Managing Shared Water Resources* (E/ESCWA/SDPD/2009/7). New York: United Nations.

_____ (2009b). *Water Development Report 3: Role of Desalination in Addressing Water Scarcity* (E/ESCWA/SDPD/2009/4). New York: United Nations.

_____ (2009c). *Increasing the Competitiveness of Small and Medium-sized Enterprises through the Use of Environmentally Sound Technologies: Assessing the Potential for the Development of Second-generation Biofuels in the ESCWA Region* (E/ESCWA/SDPD/2009/5). New York: United Nations.

_____ (2012). *Report on Intergovernmental Consultative Meeting on the Water and Energy Nexus in the ESCWA Region* (E/ESCWA/SDPD/2012/IC.1/2/Report), Beirut, 27-28 June 2012.

_____ (2014a). *ESCWA Country Profiles 2014: Key Energy Statistics* (E/ESCWA/SD/2014/Pamphlet.1). Beirut: United Nations.

_____ (2014b). *Water and Energy in the Arab Region for Sustainable Development.* Brochure produced for the occasion of World Water Day 2014, Beirut (E/ESCWA/SDPD/2014/Brochure.1).

_____ (2015a). *A Regional Agenda for the "Sustainable Energy for All" Decade in the Arab Region* (E/ESCWA/SDPD/2015/ FACT SHEET.1). Beirut (in Arabic).

_____ (2015b). *Conceptual Frameworks for Understanding the Water, Energy and Food Security Nexus - Working Paper* (E/ESCWA/SDPD/2015/WP.2).

_____ (2015c). *Natural Resources Management for Sustainable Development: The Energy-Water-Food Nexus in the Arab Region* (E/ESCWA/SDPD/2013/IG.1/4 (Part II)). Committee on Energy, Tenth Session, Amman, 22-23 March.

_____ (2015d). *Pathways towards Food Security in the Arab Region: An Assessment of Wheat Availability* (E/ESCWA/SDPD/2015/1). New York: United Nations.

_____ (2015e). *Water Supply and Sanitation in the Arab Region: Looking beyond 2015* (E/ESCWA/SDPD/2015/BOOKLET.1). Beirut: United Nations.

_____ (2015f). *Report of the Expert Group Meeting on the Water-Energy-Food Security Nexus in the Arab Region*, Amman, 24-25 March 2015 (E/ESCWA/SDPD/2015/WG.2/2/Report (28 May).

ESCWA and Federal Institute for Geosciences and Natural Resources (BGR) (2013a). *Inventory of Shared Water Resources in Western Asia* (E/ESCWA/SDPD/2013/Inventory). Beirut.

_____ (2013b). Inventory of Shared Water Resources in Western Asia: Overview, Key Findings and Outlook. Prepared in connection with the Tenth Session of the Committee on Water Resources, Beirut, 21 March.

ESCWA and League of Arab States (2013). *The Arab Millennium Development Goals Report: Facing challenges and looking beyond 2015* (E/ESCWA/EDGD/2013/1). Beirut: United Nations.

Economic Commission for Europe (ECE) (2014). Progress report on the thematic assessment of the water-food-energy-ecosystems nexus. Prepared in connection with the ninth meeting of the Working Group on Integrated Water Resources Management, 25-26 June 2014, Geneva, Switzerland. Available from http://www.unece.org/fileadmin/DAM/env/documents/2014/WAT/06Jun_25-26_Geneva/ECE_MP.WAT_WG.1_2014_6_ENG.pdf.

_____ (2015). Methodology for assessing the water-food-energy-ecosystems nexus in transboundary basins (ECE/MP.WAT/WG.1/2015/8). Prepared in connection with the tenth meeting of the Working Group on Integrated Water Resources Management, Geneva, 24-25 June 2015. Available from http://www.unece.org/fileadmin/DAM/env/documents/2015/WAT/06Jun_24-25_IWRM_Geneva/ECE_MP.WAT_WG.1_2015_8_methodology_ENG.pdf.

Eesti Energia (2008). Jordan Oil Shale Project: General Overview of the Feasibility Outcomes (3 June). Available from http://web.archive.org/web/20080603231353/http://www.jordanoilshale.net/page4.aspx.

El-Boraie, F. M., A. M. Gaber and G. Abdel-Rahman (2009). Optimizing irrigation schedule to maximize water use efficiency of Hibiscus sabdariffa under Shalatien conditions. *World Journal of Agricultural Sciences*, vol. 5, No. 4, pp. 504-514.

Embassy of Algeria to the United States of America (2015). The Algerian Agriculture Sector. Available from http://www.algerianembassy.org/economic_affairs/The_Algerian_Agriculture_Sector.html. Accessed 13 March 2015.

Energy Sector Management Assistance Program (ESMAP) (2012). *A Primer on Energy Efficiency for Municipal Water and Wastewater Utilities*. Technical Report No. 001/12. Washington, D.C.: World Bank Group. Available from http://www-wds.worldbank.org/external/default/WDSContentServer/WDSP/IB/2012/05/03/000356161_20120503035610/Rendered/PDF/682800ESMAP0WP0WWU0TR0010120Resized.pdf.

Environment (2015). How Do Fertilizers Affect the Environment. Available from www.environment.co.za/environmental-issues/how-do-fertilizers-affect-the-environment.html.

European Space Agency (2011). GlobCoverDatabase. Available from http://due.esrin.esa.int/page_globcover.php. Accessed 20 May 2015.

European Union (EU) (2012). *European Report on Development 2011/2012 - Confronting scarcity: Managing water, energy and land for inclusive and sustainable growth*. Available from http://www.erd-report.eu.

Evans, Robert, R.E. Sneed and D.K. Cassel (1996). Irrigation scheduling to improve water- and energy-use efficiencies. North Carolina Cooperative Extension Service, No. AG 452-4. Available from http://www.bae.ncsu.edu/programs/extension/evans/ag452-4.html.

Federal Ministry for Economic Cooperation and Development (BMZ) (2013). Cities and resource efficiency – the urban nexus. Factsheet. Federal Government of Germany. Available from http://www2.giz.de/wbf/4tDx9kw63gma/FactSheet_09_Nexus_engl_21052013.pdf.

Fertilizer Institute, The (2015). U.S. Fertilizer Production. Available from http://www.tfi.org/industry-resources/fertilizer-economics/us-fertilizer-production.

Fezzani, Chedli, Djamel Latrech and Ahmed Mamou (2005). The North-Western Sahara Aquifer System (NWSAS): Joint management of a transboundary water basin. *Agriculture & Rural Development*, No. 1/2005 (January). Available from http://www.docstoc.com/docs/159291681/ELR_The_North-Western_Sahara_Aquifer_System_0105.

104

Food and Agriculture Organization (FAO) (n.d.a). AQUASTAT database. Available from http://www.fao.org/nr/aquastat/. Accessed 30 March, 13 May and 1 June 2015.

_____ (n.d.b). FAOSTAT. Available from http://faostat3.fao.org/home/E. Accessed 30 March 2015.

_____ (2003). *Agriculture, food and water.* Rome. Available from ftp://ftp.fao.org/agl/aglw/docs/agricfoodwater.pdf.

_____ (2005). *The Right to Food: Voluntary guidelines to support the progressive realization of the right to adequate food in the context of national food security.* Adopted by the 127th Session of the FAO Council, November 2004. Rome. Available from http://www.fao.org/3/a-y7937e.pdf.

_____ (2006). WRI Major Watersheds of the World Delineation Database. Available from http://www.fao.org/geonetwork/srv/en/resources.get?id=30914&fname=wri_basins.zip&access=private. Accessed 20 May 2015.

_____ (2009a). Groundwater management in Saudi Arabia: Draft Synthesis Report. Rome. Available from http://www.groundwatergovernance.org/fileadmin/user_upload/groundwatergovernance/docs/Country_studies/Saudi_Arabia_Synthesis_Report_Final_Morocco_Synthesis_Report_Final_Groundwater_Management.pdf.

_____ (2009b). Declaration of the World Summit on Food Security, Rome, 16-18 November (WSFS 2009/2). Available from http://www.fao.org/fileadmin/templates/wsfs/Summit/Docs/Final_Declaration/WSFS09_Declaration.pdf.

_____ (2009c). Irrigation in the Middle East Region in Figures. FAO Reports 34. Rome.

_____ (2010). Jatropha: A Smallholder Bioenergy Crop – The Potential for Pro-Poor Development. *Integrated Crop Management Series*, vol. 8. Rome. Available from http://www.fao.org/docrep/012/i1219e/i1219e.pdf.

_____ (2011). *"Energy-smart" food for people and climate.* Issue paper. Rome. Available from http://www.fao.org/docrep/014/i2454e/i2454e00.pdf.

_____ (2013a). *Climate-smart agriculture: sourcebook.* Rome. Available from http://www.fao.org/3/a-i3325e.pdf.

_____ (2013b). AQUASTAT database: Dams. Available from http://www.fao.org/nr/water/aquastat/dams/index.stm. Accessed 20 May 2015.

_____ (2014). *The Water-Energy-Food Nexus: A new approach in support of food security and sustainable agriculture.* Rome.

FAO, International Fund for Agricultural Development (IFAD) and World Food Programme (WFP) (2013). *The State of Food Insecurity in the World: The multiple dimensions of food security.* Rome. Available from http://www.fao.org/docrep/018/i3434e/i3434e.pdf.

Forum des Chefs d'Entreprises (2013). Une étude pointe le bel avenir du gaz de schiste en Algérie (TSA). Revue de presse, p. 10. Available from http://www.fce.dz/index.php/la-veille-du-forum/category/105-revues-du-mois-doctobre?download=576:revue-de-presse-du-23-octobre-2013 (in French).

Fraunhofer Institute for Solar Energy Systems ISE (2013). *Levelized Cost of Electricity: Renewable Energy Technologies* (November). Available from http://www.ise.fraunhofer.de/en/publications/veroeffentlichungen-pdf-dateien-en/studien-und-konzeptpapiere/study-levelized-cost-of-electricity-renewable-energies.pdf.

Gleick, Peter H. (1994). Water and Energy. *Annual Review of Energy and the Environment*, vol. 19 (November), pp. 267-299.

Global Justice Now (n.d.). The six pillars of food sovereignty. Available from http://www.globaljustice.org.uk/six-pillars-food-sovereignty. Accessed 28 July 2015.

Global Risk Insights (2013). *Shale Oil Is Key to Jordan's Energy Future,* 20 May. Available from http://globalriskinsights.com/2013/05/shale-oil-is-key-to-jordans-energy-future/.

GlobCover Database. Available from http://due.esrin.esa.int/page_globcover.php. Accessed 20 May 2015.

Granit, Jakob, and John Joyce (2012). Options for cooperative action in the Euphrates and Tigris Region, Paper 20, Stockholm: SIWI. Available from http://www.siwi.org/wp-content/uploads/2015/09/Paper_20-Euphrates_and_Tigris_Region_webb.pdf.

Hafner, Manfred (2009). Domestic Energy Demand, Supply and Efficiency, Including Desalination in the Kingdom of Saudi Arabia. Study paper prepared as part of GIZ Preparatory Studies for the Ninth Development Plan in the Kingdom of Saudi Arabia, 09/2008-08/2009.

Hafner, M., Simone Tagliapietra and El Habib el Andaloussi (2012). *Outlook for Electricity and Renewable Energy in Southern and Eastern Mediterranean Countries.* MEDPRO Technical Report No. 16 (October). Available from http://www.ceps.eu/system/files/MEDPRO%20TR%20No.%2016%20Electricity%20Hafner%20et%20al.pdf.

Hardin, Garrett (1968). The Tragedy of the Commons. *Science* (14 December). Available from http://www.garretthardinsociety.org/articles/art_tragedy_of_the_commons.html.

Hélix-Nielsen, Claus, ed. (2012). *Biomimetic Membranes for Sensor and Separation Applications.* Netherlands: Springer.

Hoekstra, Arjen Y., ed. (2003). *Virtual Water Trade.* Proceedings of the International Expert Meeting on Virtual Water Trade, IHE Delft, Netherlands, 12-13 December 2002. Available from http://waterfootprint.org/media/downloads/Report12.pdf.

Hoff, Holger (2011). Understanding the Nexus. Background Paper for the Bonn 2011 Nexus Conference: The Water, Energy and Food Security Nexus. Stockholm: Stockholm Environment Institute. Available from http://www.water-energy-food.org/en/news/view__255/understanding-the-nexus.html.

Hormann, Marc, Joern C. Kuntze and Jad Dib (2012). Delivering on the Energy Efficiency Promise in the Middle East. Oliver Wyman. Available from http://www.oliverwyman.com/content/dam/oliver-wyman/global/en/files/archive/2013/Energy_Efficiency_inMiddleEastFINAL.pdf.

Human Rights Based Approach (HRBA) portal (n.d.). The Human Rights Based Approach to Development Cooperation: Towards a Common Understanding Among UN Agencies. Available from http://hrbaportal.org/the-human-rights-based-approach-to-development-cooperation-towards-a-common-understanding-among-un-agencies.

IFP Energies Nouvelles (2011). Water in fuel production: Oil production and refining. *Panorama*. Available from http://www.ifpenergiesnouvelles.com/index.php/content/download/70601/1513892/version/2/file/Panorama2011_11-VA_Eau-Production-Carburants.pdf.

Internal Displacement Monitoring Centre (2015). Syria IDP Figures Analysis. Available from http://www.internal-displacement.org/middle-east-and-north-africa/syria/figures-analysis. Accessed 24 July 2015.

International Centre for Integrated Mountain Development (2015). Contribution of Himalayan Ecosystems to Water, Energy, and Food Security in South Asia: A nexus approach. Kathmandu. Available from http://www.circleofblue.org/waternews/wp-content/uploads/2012/07/icimod-contribution_of_himalayan_ecosystems_to_water_energy_and_food_security_in_south_asia-_a_nexus_appr-1.pdf.

International Energy Agency (IEA) (2014). Key World Energy Statistics. Paris: OECD/IEA.

IEA, Energy Technology Systems Analysis Program (IEA-ETSAP) and International Renewable Energy Agency (IRENA) (2012). Water Desalination Using Renewable Energy – Technology Brief. Available from http://www.irena.org/DocumentDownloads/Publications/IRENA-ETSAP%20Tech%20Brief%20I12%20Water-Desalination.pdf.

_____ (2013). Concentrating Solar Power: Technology Brief E10. Available from https://www.irena.org/DocumentDownloads/Publications/IRENA-ETSAP%20Tech%20Brief%20E10%20Concentrating%20Solar%20Power.pdf.

International Environmental Law Research Centre (1977). United Nations Water Conference (Resolutions). In Report of the United Nations Wter Conference, Mar del Plata, 14-25 March. Available from http://www.ielrc.org/content/e7701.pdf.

International Food Policy Research Institute (IFPRI) (2002). Green revolution: Curse or blessing? Washington, D.C.: IFPRI. Available from http://thebritishgeographer.weebly.com/uploads/1/1/8/1/11812015/ib11.pdf.

International Groundwater Resources Assessment Centre (2015). Transboundary Aquifers of the World. Available from http://www.un-igrac.org/ggis/tba. Accessed 20 May 2015.

International Renewable Energy Agency (IRENA) (2014). Pan-Arab Renewable Energy Strategy 2030: Roadmap of Actions for Implementation. Available from http://www.irena.org/DocumentDownloads/Publications/IRENA_Pan-Arab_Strategy_June%202014.pdf.

International Waters Governance (n.d.). North-Western Sahara Aquifer System (NWSAS). Available from http://www.internationalwatersgovernance.com/north-western-sahara-aquifer-system-nwsas.html.

Jagannathan, N. Vijay, Ahmed S. Mohamed and Alexander Kremer (2009). *Water in the Arab world: management perspectives and innovations*. Washington, D.C.: World Bank.

Jones, M.J. (2012). *Thematic Paper 8: Social adoption of groundwater pumping technology and the development of groundwater cultures: governance at the point of abstraction.* Groundwater Governance: A Global Framework for Country Action, GEF ID 3726. Rome: FAO. Available from http://www.groundwatergovernance.org/fileadmin/user_upload/groundwatergovernance/docs/Thematic_papers/GWG_TP8_revised.pdf.

Khan, Imran (2015). Bolstering a Biofuels Market in the Middle East. Renewable Energy World.com, 5 March. Available from http://www.renewableenergyworld.com/articles/2015/03/bolstering-a-biofuels-market-in-the-middle-east.html.

Khatib, Zara (2014). Produced Water Management: A Legacy or an Opportunity for Sustainable Field Development. Society of Petroleum Engineers. Available from http://higherlogicdownload.s3.amazonaws.com/SPE/d6347f36-42f2-4203-8692-0d51d1ce0f61/UploadedImages/Zara%20Khatib%20DL%20presentation%20Oct%2029.pdf.

Khouri, Nadim, and Fidele Byringiro (2014). Developing Food Chains. In *Arab Environment No. 7: Food Security – Challenges and Prospects*, pp. 102-129. Sadik, Abdul-Karim, Mahmoud el-Solh and Najib Saab, eds. Beirut: AFED.

Kordab, Mohamad, and Maen Daoud (2011). *Water, energy and climate change nexus, prospective for the Syrian Arab Republic up to 2030: Syrian national report.* Sophia Antipolis: Plan Bleu. Available from http://planbleu.org/sites/default/files/publications/ adaptationeauenergieccsyrierapporten.pdf.

Kuuskraa, Vello A. (2013). *EIA/ARI World Shale Gas and Shale Oil Resource Assessment.* Presentation given at the 2013 EIA Energy Conference. Washington, D.C., 17 June. Available from http://www.eia.gov/conference/2013/pdf/presentations/kuuskraa.pdf.

Lamont-Doherty Earth Observatory (2015). *Did Climate Change Spark the Syrian War?* (2 March). Available from http://www.ldeo.columbia.edu/news-events/did-climate-change-help-spark-syrian-war. Accessed 17 May /2015.

Land Matrix (n.d.). Available from http://www.landmatrix.org/en/. Accessed March 2015.

League of Arab States (2004). Arab Charter on Human Rights, 22 May. Available from http://www1.umn.edu/humanrts/instree/loas2005.html.

League of Arab States, Arab Ministerial Water Council (2012). *Arab Strategy for Water Security in the Arab Region to Meet the Challenges and Future Needs for Sustainable Development 2010-2030.*

League of Arab States and Arab Organization for Agricultural Development (2007). *Strategy for Sustainable Arab Agricultural Development for the Upcoming Two Decades (2005-2025).* Available from http://www.aoad.org/strategy/straenglish.pdf.

Lindstrom, Andreas, Allan Hoffman and Gustaf Olsson (2014). Shale gas and hydraulic fracturing: Blessing or curse? *Stockholm WaterFront,* No. 1, pp. 5-7 (March). Available from http://www.siwi.org/wp-content/uploads/2015/09/WF-1-2014_web_new.pdf.

Maher, M. (2005). Computer-aided mapping irrigation scheduling for Arab Republic of Egypt. Available from http://www.icid.org/ws3_2005.pdf.

Majid, A. Hamid (2014). Technological Developments in Utilizing Unconventional Resources of Oil and Gas. Paper presented at the Tenth Arab Energy Conference, Abu Dhabi, United Arab Emirates, 21-23 December.

Mamou, A., and others (2006). North Western Sahara Aquifer System (NWSAS). In *Non-renewable Groundwater Resources: A guidebook on socially-sustainable management for water-policy makers,* Stephen Foster and Daniel P. Loucks, eds., pp. 68-74. Paris: United Nations Educational, Scientific and Cultural Organization. Available from http://www.unesco.kz/publications/sci/NonRenewableResources_en.pdf.

MapCruzin (2003). Iraq: Oil Infrastructure. Available from http://www.mapcruzin.com/free-maps-iraq/iraq_oil_2003.jpg. Last accessed 20 May 2015.

Meed Projects (2011). *The Great Man-made River project*. Available from http://www.meed.com/Journals/1/Files/2011/12/11/Sample%20Chapter.pdf.

Ministry of Water and Irrigation (2009). *Water for Life: Jordan's Water Strategy, 2008-2022*. Rev. 10.270309. Available from http://www.mwi.gov.jo/sites/en-us/Documents/Jordan_Water_Strategy_English.pdf.

_____ (2013). *Jordan Water Sector Facts and Figures*. Available from http://www.mwi.gov.jo/sites/en-us/Hot%20Issues/Jordan%20Water%20Sector%20Facts%20and%20Figures%202013.pdf.

_____ (2014). Establishing the Post-2015 Development Agenda: Sustainable Development Goals (SDG) towards Water Security - The Jordanian Perspective. Amman, Jordan (March). Available from http://www.mwi.gov.jo/sites/en-us/Hot%20Issues/SDG_Jordan%20Precspective_Post%202015.pdf.

Mirata, Murat, and Tareq Emtairah (2010). *Water Efficiency Handbook: Identifying opportunities to increase water use efficiency in industry, buildings and agriculture in the Arab world*. Beirut: Arab Forum for Environment and Development.

Mohammad, F. S., H. M. al-Ghobari and M. S. A. el-Marazky (2013). Adoption of an intelligent irrigation scheduling technique and its effect on water use efficiency for tomato crops in arid regions. *Australian Journal of Crop Science*, vol. 7, No. 3, pp. 305-313.

Moody, Charles, and others (n.d.). Desalination by Forward Osmosis. Available from www.usbr.gov/research/projects/download_product.cfm?id=726.

Moseley, Maya (2013). Unconventional Gas Beyond the US: Emerging Players in Shale Exploration and Development (September). Available from http://www.egyptoil-gas.com/publications/unconventional-gas-beyond-the-us-emerging-players-in-shale-exploration-and-development/.

Muhammad, Fatima (2014). KSA to stop wheat production by 2016. *Saudi Gazette*, 11 December. Available from http://www.saudigazette.com.sa/index.cfm?method=home.regcon&contentid=20141211227161.

Nasr, Raoul E. (2006). Water Conservation and Desert Large-scale Farming in Jordan. *Bulgarian Journal of Agricultural Science*, vol. 12, pp. 553-558. Available from http://www.agrojournal.org/12/04-08-06.pdf.

NaturalGas.org (2013). Water Requirements of Shale Production (25 September). Available from http://naturalgas.org/shale/waterrequirements/.

Nile Basin Initiative (2012). State of the River Nile Basin. Entebbe, Uganda. Available from http://nileis.nilebasin.org/content/state-river-nile-basin-report.

_____ (2013). Cooperation on the Nile. Entebbe, Uganda. Available from http://www.nilebasin.org/index.php/media-center/speeches/doc_download/26-cooperation-on-the-nile-success-story.

Observatoire du Sahara et du Sahel (OSS) (2003). *Système aquifère du Sahara septentrional: Gestion commune d'un bassin transfrontière.* Tunis (January). Available from http://www.oss-online.org/sites/default/files/fichier/rapport_de_synthese_0.pdf (in French).

Office of the United Nations High Commissioner for Human Rights (OHCHR) (1966). International Covenant on Economic, Social and Cultural Rights. General Assembly resolution 2200A (XXI) of 16 December. Available from http://www.ohchr.org/Documents/ProfessionalInterest/cescr.pdf.

Oil and Gas Journal (2014). Development planned for Libyan oil field. 17 July. Available from http://www.ogj.com/articles/2014/07/development-planned-for-libyan-oil-field.html.

Ongley, Edwin D. (1996). Control of water pollution from agriculture. FAO irrigation and drainage paper No. 55. Rome.

Organization of Arab Petroleum Exporting Countries (OAPEC) (2013). Organization of Arab Petroleum Exporting Countries Database. Available from http://oapecdb.oapecorg.org:8085/apex/f?p=112:8:0. Accessed 5 June 2015.

_____ (2014). *Annual Statistical Report*. Kuwait: OAPEC. Available from http://www.oapecorg.org/Home/Publications/Reports/Annual-Statistical-report.

Pioneer Natural Resources Company (2007). Pioneer Announces Three New Discoveries and Production Outlook for Tunisia. 18 October. Available from http://investors.pxd.com/phoenix.zhtml?c=90959&p=irol-newsArticle&ID=1064528.

Produced Water Treatment and Beneficial Use Information Center (n.d.). About Produced Water. Available from http://aqwatec.mines.edu/produced_water/intro/pw/index.htm.

Resourcematics Ltd., 2014. Resourcematics Nexus Model. http://www.resourcematics.com/water-energy-nexus/.

Richards, Alan (2001). Coping with Water Scarcity: The Governance Challenge. CGIRS Working Paper Series, No. 01-4. Santa Cruz: Center for Global International and Regional Studies, University of California. Available from https://escholarship.org/uc/item/7pv2m477.

Ricketts, Craig and Thomas Jenkins (2012). An Overview of the Practical Application of Renewable Energy Technologies to the Pumping of Ground Water for Agricultural Purposes in New Mexico. Available from http://aces.nmsu.edu/programs/sare/documents/water_confv1_1-twj-a-ricketts.pdf.

Ryan, Lisa, and Nina Campbell (2012). *Spreading the Net: The Multiple Benefits of Energy Efficiency Improvements*. International Energy Agency Insights Series. Paris: IEA.

Saif, Omar (2012). The Future Outlook of Desalination in the Gulf: Challenges and opportunities faced by Qatar and the UAE. Available from http://inweh.unu.edu/wp-content/uploads/2013/11/The-Future-Outlook-of-Desalination-in-the-Gulf.pdf.

Sakhel, Simon R, Sven-Uwe Geissen and Anne Vogelpohl (2013). Virtual industrial water usage and wastewater generation in the Middle East/North Africa region. *Hydrology and Earth System Sciences Discussions*, vol. 10, pp. 999-1039. Available from http://www.hydrol-earth-syst-sci-discuss.net/10/999/2013/hessd-10-999-2013-print.pdf.

Salem, Omar (2013). Libya's experience in the management of transboundary aquifers. In *Free Flow: Reaching water security through cooperation,* Jacqui Griffiths and Rebecca Lambert, eds. Paris: United Nations Educational, Scientific and Cultural Organization. Available from http://unesdoc.unesco.org/images/0022/002228/222893e.pdf.

Sappa, Giuseppe, and Matteo Rossi (2010). Local effects of groundwater overexploitation of the Complexe Terminal in NWSAS. Available from file:///C:/Users/258573/Downloads/N_66_Sappa_Rossi_Valencia_settembre2010.pdf.

Scheumann, Waltina, and Elke Herrfahrdt-Pähle (2008). *Conceptualizing cooperation on Africa's transboundary groundwater resources.* Bonn: German Development Institut. Available from http://www.die-gdi.de/uploads/media/Studie_32.pdf.

Sharaf, M.A., and M. T. Hussein (1996). Groundwater quality in the Saq aquifer, Saudi Arabia. *Hydrological Sciences Journal*, vol. 41, No. 5, pp. 683-696. Available from http://dx.doi.org/10.1080/02626669609491539.

Siddiqi, Afreen, and Laura D. Anadon (2011). The water-energy nexus in Middle East and North Africa. *Energy Policy,* vol. 39, No. 8, pp. 4529-4540 (August).

Struckmeier, Wilhelm, and others (2006). *WHYMAP and the World Map of Transboundary Aquifer*. Available from http://www.whymap.org/whymap/EN/Downloads/Global_maps/spec_ed_2_explan_notes_pdf.pdf?__blob=publicationFile. Sustainable Energy for All (SE4All) (2013). United Nations Decade of Sustainable Energy for All 2014-2014. Available from www.se4all.org/decade/.

United Nations (1948). Universal Declaration of Human Rights, Article 25. Available from http://www.un.org/en/documents/udhr/. Accessed 24 June 2015.

United Nations, General Assembly (1986). Declaration on the Right to Development (A/RES/41/128) (4 December). Available from http://www.un.org/documents/ga/res/41/a41r128.htm. Accessed 3 July 2015.

United Nations Human Settlements Programme UN-Habitat (2012). *The State of Arab Cities 2012/2013: Challenges of Urban Transition.* Second Edition. Nairobi (December), p.1. Available from http://www.unhabitat.org.jo/en/inp/Upload/134359_OptiENGLISH_StateofArabCities_Edited_25_12_2012.pdf. Accessed 20 June 2015.

United Nations Development Programme (UNDP) (2013). *Water Governance in the Arab Region: Managing Scarcity and Securing the Future.* New York: UNDP, Regional Bureau for Arab States.

United Nations Educational, Scientific and Cultural Organization (UNESCO) (2004). *Water Resources in the OSS Countries: Evaluation, use and management.* Paris: UNESCO. Available from http://hydrologie.org/BIB/Publ_UNESCO/SOG_OSS-CD.pdf.

_____ (2012). The Future We Want (A/RES/66/288) (11 September). Available from https://sustainabledevelopment.un.org/index.php?page=view&nr=1102&type=111&menu=35.

United Nations High Commissioner for Human Rights (UNHCR) and Food and Agriculture Organization (FAO) (2010). *The Right to Adequate Food.* Fact Sheet No. 34. Geneva: UNHCR.

United Nations Human Rights Council (2008). Resolution 7/14: The right to food (27 March). Available from http://ap.ohchr.org/documents/E/HRC/resolutions/A_HRC_RES_7_14.pdf.

United Nations University (UNU) (2013). *Water Security and the Global Water Agenda: A UN-Water Analytical Brief.* Ontario, Canada.

United States Department of Energy (2009). Concentrating Solar Power Commercial Application Study: Reducing Water Consumption of Concentrating Solar Power Electricity Generation - Report to Congress. Available from www1.eere.energy.gov/solar/pdfs/csp_water_study.pdf.

Van Berg, Caroline (2013). MENA Water, Agriculture and Rural Development. Available from https://www.houston.org/business/global/pdf/12%20WSS%20Middle%20East%20North%20Africa%20-%20Caroline%20van%20den%20Berg.pdf.

Water-technology.net (2015). As-Samra Wastewater Treatment Plant (WWTP), Jordan. Accessed 13 May 2015. Available from http://www.water-technology.net/projects/as-samra-wastewater-treatment-plant-jordan/.

WaterWatch (2006). Historic Groundwater Abstractions in the Kingdom of Saudi Arabia. Available from http://www.waterwatch.nl/fileadmin/bestanden/Project/Asia/0101_SA_2006_UNDPirrigation.pdf.

Wise Uranium Project (2014). New Uranium Mining Projects - Jordan (19 November). Available from http://www.wise-uranium.org/upjo.html.

Woertz, Eckart (2011). Arab food, water and the big Gulf land grab that wasn't. *Brown Journal of World Affairs,* vol. 18, Issue 1, p. 119. Princeton University. Available from http://connection.ebscohost.com/c/articles/85090595/arab-food-water-big-landgrab-that-wasnt.

World Bank (n.d.a). World Development Indicators. Available from http://data.worldbank.org/data-catalog/world-development-indicators. Accessed 30 March 2015.

_____ (n.d.b). World Bank Database: Renewable internal freshwater resources per capita. Available from http://data.worldbank.org/indicator/ER.H2O.INTR.PC. Accessed on 01 June 2015.

_____ (2008). Sector brief: Agriculture and rural development in MENA. Available from http://siteresources.worldbank.org/INTMENAREGTOPAGRI/Resources/AGRICULTURE-ENG-2008AM.pdf.

_____ (2012). Renewable Energy Desalination: An Emerging Solution to Close MENA's Water Gap. Washington, D.C. Available from http://water.worldbank.org/sites/water.worldbank.org/ files/publication/MENA-Desal-AGENDA-and-ABSTRACT.pdf.

_____ (2013). *Middle East and North Africa: Integration of Electricity Networks in the Arab World - Regional Market Structure and Design.* Washington, D.C. Available from: http://documents.worldbank.org/curated/en/2013/12/19777005/middle-east-north-africa-integration-electricity-networks-arab-world-regional-market-structure-design.

World Business Council for Sustainable Development (WBCSD) (2013). *Co-optimizing Solutions: water and energy for food, feed and fibre.* Available from http://www.wbcsd.org/ Pages/EDocument/EDocumentDetails.aspx?ID=16214&NoSearchContextKey=true.

World Economic Forum (2011). *Global Risks 2011, Sixth Edition: An Initiative of the Risk Response Network.* Geneva. Available from http://reports.weforum.org/wp-content/blogs.dir/1/mp/uploads/pages/files/global-risks-2011.pdf.

World Energy Council (2013). *World Energy Resources: 2013 Survey.* London. Available from http://www.worldenergy.org/publications/2013/world-energy-resources-2013-survey/.

World Food Programme (WFP) (2012). *Food security, living conditions and social transfers in Iraq - Executive Summary.* Available from http://reliefweb.int/sites/reliefweb.int/files/resources/Food %20security%2C%20living%20conditions%20and%20social%20transfers%20in%20Iraq.pdf.

World Health Organization (WHO) (2006). A compendium of standards for wastewater reuse in the Eastern Mediterranean Region (EM/CEH/142/E). Cairo: WHO. Available from http://applications.emro.who.int/dsaf/dsa1184.pdf.

WHO and UNICEF (2014). Progress on Drinking Water and Sanitation – 2014 update. Geneva: WHO/UNICEF. Available from www.who.int/water_sanitation_health/publications/2014/ jmp-report/en.

World Map (2011). Map: Syria Energy Infrastructure. Available from http://worldmap.harvard.edu/data/geonode:syria_energy_infrastructure_eia_39r.

World Meteorological Organization (1992). The Dublin Statement on Water and Sustainable Development. Adopted at the International Conference on Water and the Environment, Dublin, 26-31 January. Available from http://www.wmo.int/pages/prog/hwrp/documents/english/ icwedece.html.

World Nuclear Association (2015a). Emerging Nuclear Energy Countries (June). Available from http://www.world-nuclear.org/info/Country-Profiles/Others/Emerging-Nuclear-Energy-Countries/.

_____ (2015b). Nuclear Power in Jordan (March). Available from http://www.world-nuclear.org/info/Country-Profiles/Countries-G-N/Jordan/.

_____ (2015c). Nuclear Power in the United Arab Emirates (March). Available from http://www.world-nuclear.org/info/Country-Profiles/Countries-T-Z/United-Arab-Emirates/.

Zhu, Tingju, Claudia Ringler and Ximing Cai (2007). Energy price and groundwater extraction for agriculture: exploring the energy-water-food nexus at the global and basin levels. Available from http://www.iwmi.cgiar.org/EWMA/files/papers/Energyprice_GW.pdf.

Endnotes

1   There are 22 Arab States that are members of the League of Arab States. ESCWA is comprised of 18 Arab States, namely Bahrain, Egypt, Iraq, Jordan, Kuwait, Lebanon, Libya, Mauritania, Morocco, Oman, Palestine, Qatar, Saudi Arabia, the Sudan, Syrian Arab Republic, Tunisia, United Arab Emirates and Yemen; ESCWA assists the remaining five Arab States (Algeria, Comoros, Djibouti, Mauritania, and Somalia) through its regional cooperation with the League of Arab States and the support it provides to its associated ministerial councils.

2   FAO, n.d.a.

3   Ibid.

4   ESCWA, 2015e.

5   UN-Habitat, 2012.

6   FAO, n.d.b.

7   ESCWA, 2015d.

8   The GCC countries are Bahrain, Kuwait, Oman, Qatar, Saudia Arabia, and the United Arab Emirates.

9   World Bank, World Development Indicators. Available from http://data.worldbank.org/indicator/EG.USE.PCAP.KG.OE.

10   Ibid.

11   ESCWA, 2015a.

12   Arab Union of Electricity, 2013.

13   Hoff, 2011.

14   European Union, 2012.

15   For more information, see ECE, 2015. The ECE Convention on the Protection and Use of Transboundary Watercourses and International Lakes was adopted by ECE member States in Helsinki in 1992 and entered into force in 1996. The Convention "aims to protect and ensure the quantity, quality and sustainable use of transboundary water resources by facilitating cooperation".

16   A pilot assessment was undertaken in the Alazani/Ganik River basin. Other transboundary river basins nexus assessments were expected to be conducted in 2014-2015. See http://www.unece.org/env/water/nexus.

17   World Economic Forum, 2011.

18   ECE, FAO, IAEA, IIASA, IRENA, KTH, SEI, UNDESA, UNIDO, and WBCSD collaborated to develop such a methodology. For more information, see https://www.kth.se/en/itm/inst/energiteknik/forskning/desa/research areas/clews-climate-land-energy-and-water-strategies-to-navigate-the-nexus-1.432255.

19   Andrews-Speed, and others, 2012.

20   Federal Ministry for Economic Cooperation and Development of Germany, 2013.

21   HRBA Portal, n.d.

22   "Everyone has the right to a standard of living adequate for the health and well-being of himself and of his family, including food, clothing, housing and medical care and necessary social services, and the right to security in the event of unemployment, sickness, disability, widowhood, old age or other lack of livelihood in circumstances beyond his control." United Nations, 1948.

23   "The right to adequate food is realized when every man, woman and child, alone or in community with others, has physical and economic access at all times to adequate food or means for its procurement."

24   The Human Rights Council reaffirms "the right of everyone to have access to safe and nutritious food, consistent with the right to adequate food and the fundamental right of everyone to be free from hunger, so as to be able to fully develop and maintain his or her physical and mental capacities." United Nations Human Rights Council, 2008.

25   International Environmental Law Research Centre, 1977.

26   United Nations General Assembly resolution 64/292 on the human right to water and sanitation "recognizes the right to safe and clean drinking water and sanitation as a human right that is essential for the full enjoyment of life and all human rights".

27 Human Rights Council resolution 15/9 on human rights and access to safe drinking water and sanitation "affirms that the human right to safe drinking water and sanitation is derived from the right to an adequate standard of living and inextricably related to the right to the highest attainable standard of physical and mental health, as well as the right to life and human dignity".

28 United Nations General Assembly,1986.

29 Bradbrook and Gardam, 2006.

30 Sustainable Energy for All initiative, available from http://www.se4all.org/.

31 United Nations, 1948, Articles 25 and 26.

32 Technical efficiency is demonstrated when the output is maximized using the existing pool of resources. By contrast, economic efficiency is achieved when the cost of producing an output is minimized.

33 ESCWA and BGR, 2013a.

34 League of Arab States, 2004.

35 Ibid.

36 Ibid.

37 ESCWA, 2014b.

38 League of Arab States, Arab Ministerial Water Council, 2012.

39 League of Arab States and Arab Organization for Agricultural Development, 2007.

40 IRENA, 2014.

41 Ibid.

42 ESCWA, 2012.

43 ESCWA, 2015f.

44 Ibid.

45 ESCWA and BGR, 2013.

46 FAO, 2006.

47 FAO, 2013b.

48 ESCWA and BGR, 2013.

49 IGRAC, 2015.

50 ESCWA and BGR, 2013.

51 Ibid.

52 Ibid.

53 Ibid.

54 Granit and Joyce, 2012.

55 Ibid.

56 ESCWA and BGR, 2013.

57 Ibid.

58 Ibid.

59 Ibid.

60 Granit and Joyce, 2012.

61 Kordab and Daoud, 2011.

62 ESCWA and BGR, 2013.

63 Ibid.

64 Ibid.

65 ESCWA and BGR, 2013.

66 Lamont-Doherty Earth Observatory, 2015.

67 IDMC, 2015.

68 World Food Programme, 2012.

69 Ibid.

70 ESCWA and BGR, 2013.

71 ESCWA, 2009a.

72 Nile Basin Initiative, 2012.

73 Ibid.

74 Ibid.

75 Awulachew and others, 2012.

76 Abu-Zeid, 2008.

77 Awulachew, and others, 2012.

78 Ibid.

79 Ibid.

80 Nile Basin Initiative, 2012.

81 Awulachew, and others, 2012.

82 Ibid.

83 Nile Basin Initiative, 2012.

84 Awulachew, and others, 2012.

85 Ibid.

86 Ibid.

87 Nile Basin Initiative, 2013.

88 "Blue water" is surface and groundwater whereas "green water" is precipitation water that does not become surface water or recharged groundwater, but is stored in the soil or on top of the vegetation or soil and may later be used by plants through evapotranspiration in rain-fed agriculture, forests and natural pastures, among others.

89 Abu-Zeid, 2008.

90 ESCWA and BGR, 2013.

91 Sharaf and Hussein, 1996.

92 ESCWA and BGR, 2013.

93 Ibid.

94 Becker, 2012.

95 Ibid.

96 ESCWA and BGR, 2013.

97 Ibid.

98 Al-Ahmadi, 2009.

99 WaterWatch, 2006.

100 ESCWA and BGR, 2013.

101 Ibid.

102 Ibid.

103 Muhammad, 2014.

104 ESCWA and BGR, 2013.

105 ESCWA and BGR, 2013.

106 Nasr, 2006.

107 Ministry of Water and Irrigation, 2014.

108 Ibid.

109 ESCWA and BGR, 2013.

110 Moubidine, 2013.

111 ESCWA and BGR, 2013.

112 Ministry of Water and Irrigation, 2014.

113 Ibid.

114 Ibid.

115 World Nuclear Association, 2015b.

116 Ibid.

117 Wise Uranium Project, 2014.

118 Ibid.

119 Global Risk Insights, 2013.

120 Eesti Energia, 2008.

121 Ministry of Water and Irrigation, 2014.

122 ESCWA and BGR, 2013.

123 Ibid.

124 Ibid.

125 Ibid.

126 Ibid.

127 Ibid.

128 Ibid.

129 Besbes, and others, 2002.

130 Sappa and Rossi, 2010.

131 Scheumann and Herrfahrdt-Pähle, 2008.

132 Struckmeier, and others, 2006.

133 Scheumann and Herrfahrdt-Pähle, 2008.

134 Observatoire du Sahara et du Sahel, 2003.

135 Scheumann and Herrfahrdt-Pähle, 2008.

136 UNESCO, 2004.

137 The chotts are an area shared between Algeria and Tunis with an aggregation of playas with high evaporation and low rainfall which is subjected to sporadic ephemeral floods resulting in high salinity waters.

138 Sappa and Rossi, 2010.

139 Barrouhi, 2008.

140 Embassy of Algeria to the United States of America, 2015.

141 Salem, 2013.

142 Oil and Gas Journal, 2014.

143 Pioneer Natural Resources Company, 2007.

144 Moseley, 2013.

145 Kuuskraa, 2013.

146 NaturalGas.org, 2013.

147 Attar, n.d.

148 Forum des Chefs d'Entreprises, 2013.

149 Fezzani, Latrech and Mamou, 2005.

150 Scheumann and Herrfahrdt-Pähle, 2008.

151 Meed Projects, 2011.

152 Mamou, and others, 2006.

153 Scheumann and Herrfahrdt-Pähle, 2008.

154 Salem, 2013.

155 Scheumann and Herrfahrdt-Pähle, 2008.

156 Salem, 2013.

157 Besbes, and others, 2002.

158 International Waters Governance, n.d.

159 ECE, 2014.

160 Chouchane, and others, 2013.

161 OAPEC, 2014.

162 OAPEC, 2013.

163 IEA, 2014.

164 Hormann, Kuntze and Dib, 2012.

165 Ryan and Campbell, 2012.

166 IRENA, 2014.

167 Ibid.

168 Bryden, and others, 2013.

169 Ibid.

170 ESCWA, 2014a.

171 Arab Union of Electricity, 2013.

172 Sustainable Energy for All, 2013.

173 ESCWA, 2009c.

174 ESCWA, 2015c.

175 FAO, 2010.

176 Khan, 2015.

177 World Energy Council, 2013.

178 Majid, 2014.

179 World Energy Council, 2013.

180 Lindstrom, Hoffman and Olsson, 2014.

181 Center for Sustainable Systems, University of Michigan, 2014.

182 ESCWA, 2015c.

183 World Nuclear Association, 2015a.

184 World Nuclear Association, 2015c.

185 The Sun Belt is the region is between 40 degrees North and South of the equator, within which the entire Arab region is located.

186 Abdel Gelil, and others, 2013.

187 United States Department of Energy, 2009.

188 IEA-ETSAP and IRENA, 2013.

189 Saif, 2012.

190 Darwish, al-Najem and Lior, 2009.

191 World Bank, 2012.

192 Hafner, 2009.

193 Ibid.

194 IEA-ETSAP and IRENA, 2012.

195 Hafner, 2009.

196 IEA-ETSAP and IRENA, 2012.

197 Hagner, 2009.

198 Hélix-Nielsen, ed., 2012.

199 Moody, n.d.

200 World Bank, 2012.

201 IFP Energies Nouvelles, 2011.

202 Gleick, 1994.

203 IFP Energies Nouvelles, 2011.

204 Ibid.

205 Khatib, 2014.

206 Ibid.

207 Al Lawati, 2014.

208 Khatib, 2014.

209 Ibid.

210 Al Lawati, 2014.

211 Ibid.

212 Produced Water Treatment and Beneficial Use Information Center, n.d.

213 Khatib, 2014.

214 ESCWA, 2009b.

215 Ibid.

216 Siddiqi and Anadon, 2011.

217 Al-Zubari, 2014.

218 Siddiqi and Anadon, 2011.

219 Busche and Hayek, 2015.

220 ESCWA and BGR, 2013.

221 ESCWA, 2014b.

222 Siddiqi and Anadon, 2011.

223 Zhu, Ringler and Cai, 2007.

224 Siddiqi and Anadon, 2011.

225 Siddiqi and Anadon, 2011.

226 Ricketts and Jenkins, 2012.

227 Darem, 2015.

228 Hardin (1968) argues in this economic concept that the users of a common resource, by acting

116

naturally in an independent and selfish manner, seek to maximize their self-interest and end up depleting a common resource and thus act against what is in the best interest of the whole group, community or country.

229 Jones, 2012.
230 FAO, 2011.
231 Ibid.
232 Ibid.
233 Siddiqi and Anadon, 2011.
234 FAO, 2013.
235 Global Justice Now, n.d.
236 Arab Group for the Protection of Nature, n.d.
237 FAO, 2009a.
238 UNDP, 2013.
239 Van Berg, 2013.
240 UNDP, 2013.
241 World Bank, 2008.
242 Van Berg, 2013.
243 United Nations, 1948.
244 OHCHR, 1966.
245 ESCWA and League of Arab States, 2013.
246 Ibid.
247 Ibid.
248 Ibid.
249 Badr, 2010.
250 FAO, 2005.
251 Ibid.
252 Khouri and Byringiro, 2014.
253 IFPRI, 2002.
254 Khouri and Byringiro, 2014.
255 IFPRI, 2002.
256 Fertilizer Institute, 2015.
257 Khouri and Byringiro, 2014.
258 Beckman, Borchers and Jones, 2013.
259 Ongley, 1996.
260 Environment, 2015.
261 Ibid.
262 FAO, 2003.
263 IFAD, 2009.

264 Jagannathan, Mohamed and Kremer, 2009.
265 Evans, Sneed and Cassel, 1996.
266 Jagannathan, Mohamed and Kremer, 2009.
267 Mirata and Emtairah, 2010.
268 Mohammad, al-Ghobari and el-Marazky, 2013.
269 Dabour, 2006.
270 Dakkak, 2015.
271 Chahtech, 2013.
272 Mirata and Emtairah, 2010.

273 Ibid.
274 FAO, 2013a.
275 Ibid.
276 ESMAP, 2012.
277 Degremont Jordan, 2008.

278 Water-technology.net, 2015.
279 WHO, 2006.
280 FAO, 2013b.
281 Ibid.
282 Ibid.
283 Ministry of Water and Irrigation, 2009.
284 Ministry of Water and Irrigation, 2013.
285 Land Matrix is an online public database on land deals that endeavours to be a global and independent land monitoring initiative in order to promote transparency and accountability in decisions over land and investment.
286 Land Matrix, n.d.
287 Ibid.
288 Woertz, 2011.
289 Sakhel, Geissen and Vogelpohl, 2013.
290 Khouri and Byringiro, 2014.
291 Sakhel, Geissen and Vogelpohl, 2013.

www.ingramcontent.com/pod-product-compliance
Lightning Source LLC
Chambersburg PA
CBHW080617270326
41928CB00016B/3104